Writing is Child's Play

dyr Jim
thancs
for the
orphan
rid .

wil yootac me too
ostralyu too se coolubars

Tyler

# Writing
# Is
# Child's
# play

**Donna Reid Connell, Ed.D.**

Addison-Wesley Publishing Company

Menlo Park, California • Reading, Massachusetts • New York
Don Mills, Ontario • Wokingham, England • Amsterdam • Bonn
Paris • Milan • Madrid • Sydney • Singapore • Tokyo
Seoul • Taipei • Mexico City • San Juan

Senior Editor:            Lois Fowkes
Production Manager:       Janet Yearian
Production Coordinator:   Leanne Collins
Design Manager:           Jeff Kelly
Text Design:              Detta Penna
Cover Design:             Rachel Gage
Photographs:              Donna Connell

This book is published by Addison-Wesley's Alternative Publishing Group.

Acknowledgements: pages 33 and 34: Examples from the Kellogg Art Collection and Kellogg Drawing Hierarchy courtesy of the Golden Gate Kindergarten Association, San Francisco, California.

Orginally published as *How to Teach Your Preschooler to Write* © 1980 by Academic Therapy Publications, Inc. Published as *Writing Is Child's Play* © 1985 by AGS® American Guidance Service, Inc.

ISBN 0-201-81884-1

2 3 4 5 6 7 8 9 10-ML-98 97 96 95 94

# CONTENTS

Writing Is Child's Play summarizes the philosophy and long-term research that are the bases for the *itl Integrated Total Language Program,* a teaching curriculum that systematically implements the ideas found in this book. *Writing Is Child's Play* outlines the characteristics and learning patterns of children ages three to eight. The methods discussed are appropriate for these ages or for children functioning at these levels regardless of age.

# INTRODUCTION

## *Writing As Play*

When a young child practices an activity such as jumping rope or throwing a ball over and over for a long period of time to improve a skill, is this *play,* or is it *work?* The linguistic origin of the word *play* is related to the word *plow*, a word that implies work. Child development specialists often say, *"Play is the child's work."*

Cognitive psychologists like Jean Piaget have proven the strong relationship between play and learning (Piaget, 1969). Through play, a child learns to concentrate, to exercise imagination, and to try out ideas. Sometimes, however, teachers of young children are heard to say, "Stop playing now. We must get back to work," giving children the message that learning a skill must be work.

When we work, we assume that our efforts will be rewarded with special praise, a grade, a star on the chart, a promotion to a group with more status, or a monetary reward, such as a salary or bonus. Participating in a game of tennis for fun is play. Participating in tennis for money, or for the role of champion, is work.

Play is its own reward. Children participate in a play activity for the simple joy of it. A young child learning to walk or to climb stairs attempts the activity over and over. Doing it successfully is the prize.

An infant playing with voice noises realizes at about three months of age that he or she is making noises! This delights the infant into making them over and over. It has been said that, before their first birthday, infants from all cultures make all the noises of all the languages of the world simply by interplay of the mouth and throat parts that produce sound (Travis, 1978).

Between their first and second birthdays, young children combine voice noises into nonsense syllables and say them in the rhythm of the language they hear around them (Aitchison, 1976). Many Chinese words change their meaning through variation in voice pitch. In imitation, Chinese toddlers babble in this singsong rhythm. Most American children babble in the less varied pitch and rhythm of English. When a child at this stage plays with a toy telephone, it is possible to interpret the end of a sentence or question from the rise and fall of the child's voice, even though the sounds have no meaning. This is language play.

Gradually children concentrate only on the speech sounds they hear in the parent culture; these are the ones that are rewarded with interest and praise. Sounds from other languages disappear from their repertoire. Adults begin to attach meaning to these first syllables, and true, meaningful language emerges. We accept its simplicity and are amused by its errors. We celebrate "ma-ma" and "da-da." Grandma celebrates "na-na," and Grandpa celebrates "papa." We do not expect "mother" from beginners. We praise their efforts even though young children do not talk like adults at this stage.

At this crucial point language does not emerge through simple maturation, like a second set of teeth or adolescent sexual characteristics. It takes another person—an older child, a parent, a caregiver, or a teacher—interacting verbally with the child for meaningful language to have its best development.

Like oral language, written language also has its beginning play stages. Early writing play lays the foundation skills for later writing. As with speech, interaction with an adult is necessary for writing "babble" to move to the next stage of meaningful written communication. Expecting beginning writers to function like adults, with elaborate letter formation or dictionary-correct spelling, will lead to frustration for both children and adults. Elaborate letters and correct spelling aren't necessary for beginning writing to take place.

The major role of a beginning writing tutor, whether parent, teacher, or other caregiver, is to carefully prepare an environment that encourages the young child to scribble, draw, or write. When young children are given an opportunity to choose scribbling, drawing, and writing as a preferred play activity, they will practice it happily and feel joy and growth in their ability to *begin* participating in written communication.

The second role of the adult is to show interest in the child's natural scribbling growth and to watch for the appearance of simple letter shapes as they appear in the child's designs. These shapes appear in a child's scribbling "accidentally," in the same way a child produces the first oral "mama." When a child draws a letter shape, an adult should tell the child the meaning for what he or she has made.

For example, when the vertical-horizontal cross appears in the child's scribblings, usually around the fourth birthday, the adult should tell the child that he or she has made a "/t/,"* using the sound, not "tee" or "tuh." /t/ is the symbol for the last sound in *cat*. That is the information the child needs in order to learn to write and to read.

If their first written "letter" symbol is celebrated and perhaps hung in a prominent place and admired, children will usually repeat this act again and again, each time saying the speech sound. When this happens, the adult has helped lay the foundation for understanding that alphabet letters are simply outline drawings representing noises that we make with our voices. If the adult "jumps the gun" by drawing a cross for the child to imitate or by simply showing the child a letter *t* and saying, "This is a *tee*," the child does not experience the joy of discovery. Young children learn best by doing, not by looking or listening. When a child has drawn a cross, she or he is ready to begin associating sounds and symbols.

The easiest time to teach the correspondence between letters and their speech sounds is when the brain centers controlling the growth of oral language are still rapidly maturing. Usually this is up to the fifth birthday (Koffka, 1959). This is also the time of life when young children's interest in speech sounds is at its peak. (For adults who want to help young children with these basic prephonics skills, there is an easy-to-follow guide in the Phonics section of Part 2.)

---

*When letters are enclosed in slashes in the text, they refer to the *speech* sounds represented by the letters. When letters are italicized in the text, they refer to alphabet letter *names* such as *a, b, c.*

The closed line usually appears in children's scribblings about the third birthday, when children have developed sufficient neurological control to stop a spiral scribble (Beery, 1981). Parents often greet this major milestone by praising the child for making a "circle," a "ball," or a "balloon." It is more useful to hail this symbol with, "You made an 'ah' "(not an "oh"). For example, tell the child that he* has made a picture of the noise the doctor tells you to make when she wants to look in your throat. Then take the child to a mirror and show him that his mouth is big and round when it makes that noise. In this case the lips form the same shape as the picture of the noise. Guide the child's finger around his lips so that he can feel the roundness. Draw a cartoon face with a wide-open mouth and add a "talking balloon." Put a circle inside the balloon and tell the child that the cartoon person is saying "ah."

The speech sound, "ah," as in the word *on*, is the major sound represented by the letter *o* in the English language (Dewey, 1970). When a child finds an *o* on cereal boxes or in picture books and says she or he has found an "ah," the child will be correct about one-third of the time. If, on the other hand, a child is told, "You made an *o*," using its alphabet name as in the word *home*, the child would be correct only about one-seventh of the time. Knowledge of alphabet letter names is not a useful tool for beginners; letter names can be learned at a later stage.

The letter *o* represents many different speech sounds in the English language (*on, off, no, to, good, ton, women*). Teaching young children more than one of these sounds at a time may cause confusion and disinterest. It makes more sense to help the child learn the most frequently used speech sound first—the one needed most often in primary-level reading and writing. Children have a wonderful time practicing this newfound knowledge. They will find "ah's" all over: on signs, on cereal boxes, in the newspaper, on license plates. They will draw the letter with a stick in the sandpile, with a finger in the pudding, with a brush and a pail of water on the fence or sidewalk.

This is writing play!

---

*In *Writing Is Child's Play* the use of feminine and masculine pronouns is varied. However, the information presented applies to girls and boys alike.

## Writing As Communication

*Writing*, in this book, doesn't refer to any particular form of letters made with separate strokes or continuous lines or joined into words. Herein, writing means human communication by means of visible marks, or the expression of ideas using written words. In order to perform this act of writing, a person must

- *form characters or letters on the surface of some material* using an instrument, such as a stick in wet sand or clay or a finger in pudding or paint.
- *imprint letters on a surface* using ready-formed rubber stamps, home-made stamps, a typewriter, or a computer.
- *string already-formed letters together into words,* using alphabet blocks, magnetic letters, wooden letters, or similar letter tools.

All of these are simple acts of writing. Educators call writing *encoding*—putting the noises we make when we talk into code form. If we want to share our thoughts widely, we use a common code known to all who are literate in our language. The common code for English we call the *alphabet*.

The aim of this book is to guide adults in helping young children make and use alphabet letters so that they can eventually communicate with others in writing. In order to do this, children need to learn three basic skills:

- to make alphabet letters
- to associate speech sounds with the letters they represent
- to follow the top-to-bottom, left-to-right patterns of written English.

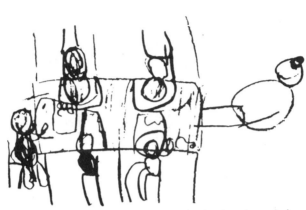

Michael.

i lic to rit StoreS
at Scol. i dro
pichrS to.

# PART 1

# NURTURING CHILDREN'S NATURAL DRIVE TO WRITE

## *Sharing the Joy of Accomplishment*

The single most important reason for helping young children learn to write is that both adults and children receive an emotional high in the process. Every time children achieve a major milestone in growth, they make a significant spurt forward in autonomy—exercising control over their environment. There are strong natural drives in the healthy child to be independent, to "do it myself."

One of these drives peaks about the fourth birthday in the average child. It happens regardless of the child's home base, be it in Kansas City, Tokyo, or Tibet. At about four, young children have a drive to imitate the drawn and written symbols of their parent culture. They want to make the signs and designs they see in their daily life. This drive is so strong that, unless adults provide an approved outlet for it, children will scribble on walls, floors, or furniture even if they know they will be punished! This natural drive is documented in Rhoda Kellogg's massive, long-term study of young children's drawings (Kellogg, 1970). The Kellogg files in San Francisco have over a million drawings by children from both primitive and sophisticated cultures all over the world. Kellogg believed that the teaching of reading and writing has never capitalized on every child's natural interest in abstract symbols (McBroom, 1968).

Montessori also observed children's natural drive to write at an early age. She suggested that if adults could learn writing as easily as children, illiteracy could he abolished in one month (Montessori, 1967). "Two obstacles would prevent such a brilliant success. Adults do not have that enthusiasm which is produced in children by their psychic sensitivities, and which is present only during that natural constructive period when language is learned." She also said that an adult's hand is too stiff to easily acquire the delicate movements necessary for writing.

Alphabet letters surround American children, from the labels on their shirts to television commercials. What they see is what they try to copy. After a preliminary period of trying to copy letters in response to this natural drive, children's curiosity usually spurs them to ask, "What did I write?" or "What does this say?" If the child has written something like *ot*, adults should translate exactly what the child has made ("aht"). It is important to give as much importance to nonsense words like *ot* as to actual words, such as *to* or *hot*. Meaningful written words will follow after this first "babbling" stage. Adults must give correct information at the babbling phase, just as they do with oral language, for further growth to take place. When at last children can write a simple message that someone else can read, their joy in accomplishment is unbounded!

When adults encourage children's natural drive to learn, they receive great pleasure in sharing this "secret" code. They not only share their children's delight in accomplishment, but they know that they are carrying on a 3000-year-old tradition of civilization: alphabetic language. Young fathers in my college classes have told me that they felt like the less important parent until they started helping their children learn to write. The shared pleasure of parent and child brought to the union a closeness not previously experienced.

## Writing As a Survival Skill

Another major reason for teaching writing to young children is writing's place of importance in our word-laden American culture. Parents in urban areas usually teach their children how to survive in heavy traffic. Parents living near deep water usually realize the importance of early swimming lessons. In today's world the ability to communicate with others *in writing* is also a major survival skill. Without it, a person is forever disabled.

Children who can independently write letters and words will usually be successful in primary school. In later years when progress is so dependent on test scores in reading or math, children are usually expected to *write* the answers. Students who cannot write fluently and legibly will not get credit for what they know.

When young people apply for a job or for a college scholarship, those making the decisions are often more influenced by legible answers on an application than by anything else. Also, future promotion in the world of work may often be seriously affected by one's ability or inability to put thoughts in writing.

## What's Happened to Writing in American Schools?

At the turn of the century one common reading method was called the Alphabetic Method. Beginners were taught to name alphabet letters and then to memorize a beginning vocabulary by spelling words aloud (M-O-T-H-E-R—"mother"). Results of this method indicated that it was not a strong way to teach young children to read. When educators were then told by supervisors not to use the Alphabetic Method, many teachers and administrators misunderstood the directive to mean, "Don't teach alphabet letters," and began to de-emphasize writing.

Two decades later a whole-word reading method invented for deaf children began to be used for all American children. Publishers developed basal reading programs using this whole-word technique. After a certain number of whole words were memorized, then word analysis by component letters was taught. This reading method served to make writing development seem less important for beginners. Independent composition of sentences was not expected until the middle of second grade (Chall, 1983).

Another historical reason for the de-emphasis on teaching writing occurred when the Soviets blasted Sputnik into outer space in 1957. The American public panicked and demanded that educators upgrade their math and science teaching to insure that we could compete in the space race. Teacher training until the 1980s emphasized math and reading, but not writing.

## The New Approach to Writing

When American educators imported the Australian concept of Whole Language (Holdaway, 1979), teachers began to teach writing and reading simultaneously to beginners. The basal reader approach was replaced with real literature.

Work at the University of New Hampshire (Graves and Stuart, 1985) was primarily responsible for a renewed surge in the interest of teaching writing to beginners. Graves' early work with first graders has spread throughout the nation. Now it is not unusual to expect youngsters to begin journals on their first day of kindergarten, even if their first pages are only scribbles.

## Parents as Teachers

A New Zealander (Clay, 1987) suggests that writing begin even earlier, before kindergarten, with parents as teachers. Japanese parents also begin helping their young children to

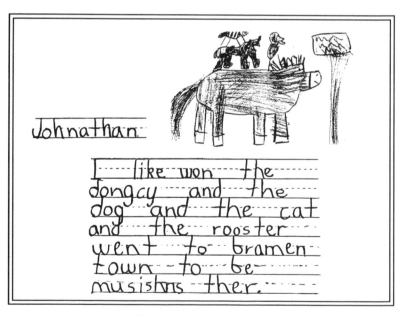

Johnathan (5) enjoys writing book reports, even though he cannot read books yet.

Nick (5) enjoys following his whole language
activities with writing.

Angelina (5) cannot read *Peter Pan*, but she
can write a book report about it.

write the simplified symbols of their language, beginning as early as age 3 when the main circuitry of the brain is being formed (Ibuka, 1980). They use brush and waterbased black paint or markers to imitate lines, angles and curves on a plain surface. It has been suggested that this exploratory practice also gives Japanese children a head start in math as well as literacy.

Parents sometimes say "I'm not good at teaching my own child," when it is obvious that they have successfully taught many social and academic skills such as talking, eating with tools, and counting to their children. Problems arise when parents separate "play" skills from "school" skills. When they teach their children to talk and to eat with tools, perfection is not expected. Children are encouraged at first to play at talking and eating, to play at counting. Mistakes are expected— even enjoyed and celebrated.

One of the values of preschool writing is that both adults and children can treat it as exploratory play with written language. First lessons should be short and should cease when the child no longer shows interest or enthusiasm—as soon as the activity is no longer play.

At the same time parents or teachers of young children should not continue to accept errors in talking or writing as correct. Eventually young children need to learn that "wa-wa" will not be acceptable talk when they are thirsty in kindergarten. Similarly, adults should gradually correct children who continue to make letters upside down, backward, or with inefficient stroke sequences. Otherwise these habits will become so ingrained that they will be very difficult to correct later on.

Any correcting of letters should be made in the same spirit as we assist young children in acquiring speech. For example, if a child tells us, "I jumpted," we don't usually say, "You said it wrong." Instead we simply repeat the child's words in the more acceptable form, "Yes, you jumped." Gradually the child will begin using the adult's language.

When correcting letter formation the adult could say, "This is how I make that letter," demonstrating its sequence of strokes. Then the adult could model the letter by drawing it in the air and encouraging the child to do so in imitation. Any instruction should be fun for the child.

If the *itl* letter-animal stories have been read to the child, a simple reminder such as, "*Piggy* lives at the farm. Remember that all the farm animal letters begin with a stick line," will be sufficient. Further discussion of letter formation can be found in the section headed *Preparing a Writing Environment,* page 21.

Invented spelling, on the other hand, should be not only accepted, but celebrated. Requiring beginners to use dictionary-correct spelling will retard both spelling and writing growth. Children will restrict their writing to only the words they know how to spell. A further discussion of invented spelling can be found in Part 2, page 97.

## *Meaning First or Phonics First?*

Meaning and phonics support each other, especially when children are first learning the language. Speech sounds and language comprehension are interwoven thoughout the early years for maximum development of emerging literacy. Neither meaning nor phonics should be neglected in favor of the other.

The natural steps are developmental. Interest in speech sounds or comprehension depends on different maturity levels. During their first year, infants try out at least one hundred speech sounds from all the spoken languages of the world. The sounds are pure invention, as infants vary the position of their own mouth and throat parts and delightedly realize that they are making the sounds themselves. Later, when parents notice that their infants are accidentally beginning to combine a consonant sound and a vowel sound into a repeated syllable *(mama, dada),* the parents excitedly asume the meaning. Family celebrations of spoken "words" cause young children to repeat the special combinations of sounds. Meaning takes over.

Toddlers' memory repetitions of rhymes and stories read to them are primarily joyful noise. Later, when young children pick up a book and retell the story aloud in their own words as they pretend to read, meaning becomes paramount.

When preschool and kindergarten children begin to acquire alphabet skills and play with invented spellings, they listen to the sequential speech sounds in a word before writing letters representing the sounds they hear. This auditory first step is evident in invented spellings that record immature speech patterns: *dis* for *this*, *wiv* for *with* or *sitn* for *sitting*. Later, when reading happens, meaning takes precedence.

Most phonics programs for beginners, both those designed for young children and those designed for teaching adult illiterates, use key words and pictures for extracting their beginning sounds and associating them with alphabet letters. A recent research summary (Goswami and Bryant, 1990) indicates that "Some time before children begin to learn to read they hear and produce rhyme. They become adept at recognizing when words have common rhymes or common onsets." The term *onset* refers not just to the first sound in a word. It can be a sequence of sounds in the beginning, such as the common onsets in *string* and *strip*. This research is strong evidence that endings of words are equal to their beginnings when teaching nonreaders.

We know that some young children teach themselves to read without any understanding of our alphabetic system. It is impossible, however, to write messages that someone else can understand unless one has some knowledge about how the alphabetic code works.

In Australia and New Zealand, where Whole Language was developed, parents usually provide their children with an understanding of the alphabetic code. Many children in these two countries enter kindergarten with sufficient alphabet skills for independent writing with invented spelling. I have observed children in New Zealand and Australia on their first day of kindergarten writing paragraphs with three and four sentences.

Other than helping their children memorize the alphabet rhyme, American parents usually do not show them the relationship between speech sounds and alphabet letters so that children can write. To make Whole Language work effectively here, our schools must supply this missing ingredient.

In extensive observations of American schools (Chall, 1967, updated 1983) it was noted that children are usually not expected to produce independent compositions until the middle of second grade. Today, however, with more emphasis on writing in our schools, there has been a renewed interest in teaching the speech sounds associated with alphabet letters (Adams, 1990). Adams stresses the importance of "phonemic awareness" as a strong predictor of reading success.

Phonemic awareness is the ability to think consciously about the sound structure of words. Young children have acquired phonemic awareness when they have an understanding that their speech is composed of individual sounds. This awareness of speech sounds can be developed through amusing game-like language activities. One activity might be to read aloud literature selections dealing playfully with the sounds of language through repetition, rhyme and alliteration. Young children enjoy repeating these strings of speech noises. It is important that adults understand this difference between reading *to* children and reading *with* children as a participatory experience.

## Writing Before Reading

Yaden and Templeton (1986) have reported on a study in France and another long large-scale study in Holland comparing the difficulty between writing and reading for beginners. Young children were asked to synthesize speech sounds into whole words and to do the opposite task, analyze whole words into their component speech sounds. Researchers first gave beginners the syllables in a familiar word, such as *ham-bur-ger,* and asked them to say it rapidly, turning it into a known word, *hamburger.* This is synthesis. At another time researchers used the same test vocabulary, but this time they gave the children whole words and asked them to say the words slowly, breaking them into syllables orally. This is analysis. The interesting results showed that synthesis is easier for beginners than analysis. In other words, beginning writing, a synthesis task, is easier than beginning reading, an analysis task.

Some researchers have studied the strong natural drive to write that is so evident in young children (Durkin, 1972). These studies show that children who teach themselves to read with little or no formal instruction are often early writers as well. Montessori told us at least seventy-five years ago that writing is easier than reading, and that preschool writers naturally "explode spontaneously into reading" (Lillard, 1972). We have no evidence that this same kind of explosion occurs with six- or seven-year-olds. The evidence suggests that their neurological peak, their natural drive for writing, which Montessori called the "sensitive" period, has already passed.

A school art specialist working primarily with African American children in Washington D.C. believes that children are not ready to read until their drawings show linear development—when their people and objects stop floating in outer space on the page and rest on a ground line (Platt, 1977). Writing in a left-to-right pattern assists this development of linearity. Her research points up the need for more drawing as foundation for reading as well as writing.

Writing teaches young children that written English is a system of symbols, like math. Letters have sound values in the same way that numerals have number values. We usually teach beginners the number values to 9. Then, as a harder task, we teach that numerals have different place values, depending upon their position in the number; thus 12 is not 21. Similarly, the letter *o* changes its sound value in our language depending upon its position in a syllable (*on* is not *no*).

It takes about two years (six months to about two and a half years of age) for most young children to carry on a meaningful conversation. In the same way, it takes about two years for young children to learn to write meaningful messages (from three to five, four to six, five to seven, or six to eight). Rushing the process by trying to compress it into a shorter period of time leads to confusion and possibly fear of failure. That is the risk of waiting until first grade to begin teaching children to make symbols. Pressures from the public, parents, and educational administrators then tend to push teachers into trying to compress two years of beginning writing instruction into one.

## Developing Thinking Skills

Two major factors affect a child's readiness for writing: nature and nurture. There are children who mature slowly, those who mature rapidly, and those whose pace is in between. Each person has his or her own built-in time clock.

Adults cannot change children's natural rate of maturation. They can, however, influence a child's writing readiness through teaching or nurturing. Some children will never be six-footers, regardless of special diet or exercise. On the other hand, a poor diet *can* affect eventual adult height. Similarly, parents and teachers can encourage readiness to write by helping children develop the necessary thinking skills.

A skill is something we practice until we are proficient. Thinking skills are the habits that a person has acquired by using her or his mind in particular ways until the mental responses become almost or completely automatic. If these thinking skills are efficient, the solutions to problems will be easier to find.

Five thinking skills that prepare children to write can be stimulated in the preschool years. An easy way to remember the names of these skills is to think of the word SLIDE, an acronym for Sequence, Language, Identicality, Directionality and Equivalence. Game activities can be planned to enhance these skills in young children. They are interrelated, but need not be developed in any special order (Connell, 1990).

If, on the other hand, any one of them is undeveloped, a child's ability to learn to write could be seriously affected. Development and stimulation of these skills is too important to leave to chance.

**Sequence** is simply understanding that some things need to go in a special order. Montessori wrote that there is a natural drive for order between the second and third birthdays (Gitter, 1969). It is important to stress order at this particular time of life. For example, following a familiar schedule and showing two-year-olds how to put toys or clothes away are activities that help to develop a sense of order. Children whose sequencing skills are weak will not be able to make strokes of single letters in order or to write letters in words in correct order.

Sequence is related to the ideas of *same* and *different*. A series is just a chain of differences. These differences can be detected by carefully looking, listening, or feeling. The differences may also be related to a special time order, such as first, second, or third.

Helping young children to retell a short story will develop a feeling for sequence. Stringing beads in a pattern, learning the steps in making a sandwich, or helping to guide a driver on a familiar route are all activities that develop sequencing.

**Language** begins with the first birth cry. About the third month of life a child makes the exciting discovery that the noises she hears are coming out of her own mouth! If parents imitate their baby's voice noises and regularly carry on a conversation with the baby, the infant will be encouraged to continue exploring sounds to see how many different vocal noises she can make.

Infants will carefully study an adult's mouth to see how a speech sound is made. They will imitate the position of lips, tongue, and teeth. During this important language development period, from birth to school age, it is helpful to face young children when talking to them. Bending down to a child's level to speak makes it easier for the child to imitate single sounds or words. Showing a young child that the teeth are closed and the tongue is not peeping out will help prevent lisping. A shy child will sometimes imitate sounds or words more willingly if the speaker uses a mirror—the child may be more comfortable imitating a reflection.

Very rapid adult speech is difficult for beginners to copy (Winitz, 1969). For example, watching a British television program will demonstrate that oral British English is much more rapid than American English. Americans have to listen very carefully to understand British English. Young children have the same problem when trying to copy the rapid speech of parents or teachers. Such attempts tend to cause them to substitute one speech sound for another and to delete parts of words. Baby talk may sound cute, but inability to distinguish fine differences in speech sounds often leads to later problems in making written symbols to represent those sounds—the letters and words in writing, as well as reading. For example, school-age children, who still count "one, two, free" may have a difficult time distinguishing between words with the letters *f* and *th*.

In addition to articulation, children's comprehension and their use of words grow rapidly during the preschool years. One of the best ways to expand vocabulary is through reading not *to* but *with* young children. Squirmy children will sit for longer reading periods if they are encouraged to participate by talking about the story and by pointing to parts of the pictures or to letters they have learned. They need to be actively involved. Asking children, "What do you think will happen next?" is a good way to involve them. Also, when reading a rhymed story, the adult can stop at the second rhymed word and let a child try to supply the word. After a bit of practice children will learn that the expected word must have the same ending syllable and also must make sense in the story.

Many Big Books developed for Whole Language programs assist in these activities.

**Identicality** means understanding that some things are exactly the same as other things. Sameness is easier to understand than *not the same*, or *different*. The young child needs to learn that when we find twin things we say they are the *same* or *alike*. When teaching identicality, it is important not to confuse a young child with items that are just similar, or are simply used for the same purpose. They must be identical in every way (same color, size, flavor, etc.) or they do not match. A green jelly bean can only be matched with another green jelly bean. A lion animal cracker is only identical to another lion animal cracker.

**Directionality** refers to our knowledge of where we are in space, and where we are going. Without a solid understanding of spatial relationships such as up-down, front-back, and left-right, young children will experience extreme difficulty in learning to read, write, and spell. Written language has specific directionality patterns.

No child is born with an awareness of the space surrounding her body. This spatial environment begins to make sense as the tactile (touch) and the kinetic (motion) sensory mechanisms feed back into the brain the results of personal movement experience. Active exercise and learning to control body movement will lead to a knowledge of directionality.

Since writing is essentially an upper-body act, care needs to be taken that exercise include the upper back, shoulders, and arms. Leg exercise, such as riding a tricycle, doesn't help to develop the arms and back. A young child who cannot sit comfortably on the floor for extended periods of time without leaning back on the hands for props or without folding the lower legs back for support usually is showing evidence of weak upper-back muscles. This child will later tire quickly in drawing or writing activities—upper-body tasks. Push-ups, pull-ups, climbing, and hanging on the bars will help to develop stronger backs, arms, and shoulders.

Some schoolchildren who need extra help to learn basic reading and writing may be children who started standing and walking at an early age (Delacato, 1970). These children have often skipped the crawling period in infancy. Later, in crawling games, these school-age children must concentrate intensely in order to alternate left and right hands, and at the same time, alternate opposite right and left knees. Their running patterns are awkward and they often have major difficulty learning to skip on alternate feet.

It may be that several months of crawling exercise during infancy develops the left-right awareness needed for efficient reading and writing. This suggests that early standing or walking should not be encouraged.

If a preschooler or school-age child still cannot crawl in a smooth alternating pattern, it is possible to fill in that gap in neurological development by playing crawling games with the child. At first it may be necessary to actually move the child's arms and legs in alternate synchrony. When the pattern comes more easily, playing crawl-catch—rolling a soft ball so the child must crawl to it—will provide practice. As the crawl pattern becomes smoother, crawling races on a soft surface can be used.

Some researchers doubt the validity of the Delacato study. My own experience as a reading specialist suggests ties to letter-and word-reversal problems when a child misses the crawling stage. For example, one of my students, an obviously intelligent six-year-old who is struggling with writing and reading reversals, had been placed very early in a walker with wheels. This child walked alone at eight months, but his crawling period was bypassed.

**Equivalence** grows out of the development of both language and identicality and is the hardest of the thinking skills to learn. It should not be taught until children can match objects exactly. *Equivalence* requires that a young child understand that two or more things are not identical, but they have the same value for a particular reason. They may be the same color, size, or shape. They fit in the same category. They may be used for the same purpose.

Foundations for equivalence can be laid with sorting games, block play, and simple cooking experiences when one food is substituted for another. Children need to be told why one thing can take the place of another: for example, two small blocks for one large block.

Part of the difficulty in distinguishing between equivalence and identicality lies in the English language: the word *same* means both *identical* and *equivalent*. To add to the confusion, when adults substitute the word *alike* for the word *same*, some children believe that they are being asked whether or not they *like* the object.

Some reading specialists believe that children's minds are not sufficiently developed for reading until they demonstrate an understanding of equivalence, or what Piaget has called *conservation*. These specialists would postpone the teaching of reading until a child is six and a half or seven years old.

It *is* wise to postpone reading instruction until this thinking stage is reached. However, children who write early usually explode into reading spontaneously. It is possible that the act of writing—substituting letters for speech sounds— develops the understanding of equivalence, or conservation, earlier.

When trying to write a message independently or to write words from dictation in the first years of school, young children will be more successful if these basic thinking skills—*Sequence, Language, Identicality, Directionality,* and *Equivalence*—have been developed prior to school entrance.

## Preparing a Writing Environment

If the child's physical surroundings are planned so that she or he can freely choose to play with items that help build writing readiness, the child cannot help but grow in these skills.

As soon as an infant can hold a spoon, he or she has developed the neurological readiness to begin to hold other tools. When the child can look into a bowl of food, independently fill the spoon, and guide it to the mouth, it indicates that the child's eyes and hands are beginning to coordinate.

By the first birthday or before, a washable, nontoxic felt-tipped pen can be placed in the infant's hand. If a big piece of paper is taped to the highchair tray, the child can be shown that scribbles magically appear when the hand with the pen is moved against the paper. A black, felt-tipped pen is best for catching attention. It will make marks with the least pressure. When young children begin to watch their own scribbling, they will gradually come to realize that they are making the marks independently. This is similar to infants getting pleasure out of vocal play when they discover they are making the noises they hear. The major supervision task at this point is to show children that the writing tool does not go into the mouth like a spoon. First lessons in scribbling should probably not last longer than a minute or two. After that the fun goes out of it for both infant and adult, and it becomes work, not play.

Austin shows interest in his own beginning scribbles.

One-or two-year-old children are more interested in the scribbling activity itself than in any product. Toddlers don't know or care what they are making. Their first abstract designs will gradually develop over the new few years. Parents or other caregivers who save and date these samples, making a file or placing these first designs in an album, can refer to them with the child to observe this gradual growth. Adding a snapshot now and then will further emphasize the growth and change.

When a child can stand and walk steadily, taping large sheets of paper to a wall or to a refrigerator door will encourage more scribbling practice. An old newspaper will do, especially the want-ad sheets, which have no dark headlines. Sometimes local newspapers will save the ends of their rolls of newsprint for customers. Obviously, young children should not have unsupervised use of scribbling tools or they will

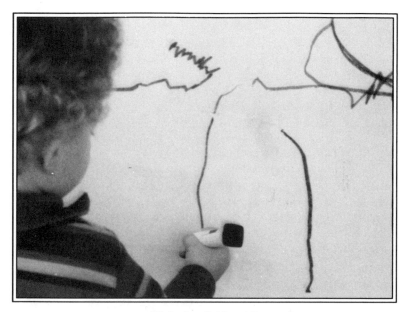

Nicholas Seifert (2)

scribble on everything in sight. Adults should be on hand to watch the scribbling for a short time daily, keeping felt-tipped pens, paints, and crayons out of reach at other times.

When a young child scribbles standing up, the first vertical lines will appear early. These will be made top-to-bottom, simply obeying the natural law of gravity. Later these top-to-bottom strokes will lead to making alphabet letters easily and correctly.

On the other hand, if first scribbling is done sitting at a table or desk, the first verticals will likely be made from bottom to top. The young, egocentric child is the center of his or her own universe. Movements are learned from the body outward. Children who habitually scribble in this way, bottom-to-top, will have major difficulty in breaking the habit in order to learn efficient writing strokes when they enter school. The best way for teachers to remediate these children later is to go back to having them do their writing in an upright position, at an easel or at a chalkboard, until the top-to-bottom habit has become natural. It's important for teachers and parents to cooperate in teaching these writing skills. Children will make slow progress if they write top-to-bottom at school and bottom-to-top at home.

For preschool children, paper and a black writing tool are preferable to a dark chalkboard and light chalk. The latter give the reverse image, like the negative of a photograph, and can cause visual confusion (Furst, 1979). Later, when children can make letters and numerals correctly, chalkboards are excellent for practice. Wipe-off boards with white surfaces are an alternative to chalkboards. These require easy-off crayons or special wipe-off pens available at most stationery stores. These boards, however, require very close supervision or the surface can easily be ruined with the wrong kinds of crayons or markers. Pieces of laminated plastic counter top—cutouts from the holes for sinks—are also excellent writing surfaces; these may be available from a local kitchen cabinet maker. Wipe-off or washable felt pens will work on the plastic surface.

Tiffany practices her vertical/horizontal cross.

If the child is using chalk and a chalkboard, putting a large, old sock on the nondominant hand to use as an eraser will help prevent chalkdust from irritating the nose. Wearing the sock also helps some children remember which hand is their writing hand. The socks should be washed frequently to remove the dust. Socks are also useful with wipe-off boards. A damp sponge will erase washable markers.

When children are habitually making top-to-bottom verticals, they can then scribble and draw in a seated position. Very young children still need to have the paper taped to a tabletop. Children should be taught as soon as possible, however, that drawing or writing is a two-handed process. One hand holds the writing tool and the other steadies the paper. Some children are slow in learning to make horizontal lines because they are constantly changing the position of the paper. They will, for example, when making a cross, or a letter *t*, make the first vertical stroke, then turn the paper and make a second vertical crossing the first. This habit will certainly slow development of writing fluency. If you observe your child changing the position of the paper, tape it to the tabletop, even if the child is of school age.

The efficient grasp of an eating tool, such as a fork or spoon, is identical with the efficient grasp of a writing tool, crayon, marker or pencil. This prehensile grasp—using the opposable thumb—is unique to the human race. The opposable thumb made it possible for our prehistoric ancestors to become tool users. Before infants develop neurologically to the point at which they can use their opposable thumbs, they will hold a spoon or rattle in the whole fist, like a weapon.

When parents or other caregivers do not make the effort to help older children change to the more efficient grasp of an eating tool, then those children will have a difficult time later learning to hold a writing tool for fluency. Their letters will be slowly drawn, rather than written.

Figure 1

These steps describe the writing grasp:

1. The tool is held by the thumb, index, and middle finger approximately one inch above the writing point— the efficient three-point grasp.
2. The tool rests primarily on the near side of the middle finger, just below the first joint.
3. The end of the thumb is placed on the other side of the tool, opposite the middle finger.
4. The end of the index finger rests on the top surface of the tool, between the other two fingers.

You can use a felt-tipped pen to put marks on children's fingers to remind them where the special grasping areas are and which fingers should touch the writing tool. If necessary, also put a strip of colored tape on the writing tool to remind children where to grasp it. A soft plastic, triangular sleeve slipped on the tool may help. Children need to be shown how to rest their writing hand and arm on the table when drawing and writing.

The furniture in the writing environment needs to fit children. Chairs should be low enough so children's feet will rest comfortably on the floor. Even more important, tabletops should not be higher than a child's navel or bent elbow. If children have to raise their arms to draw or write, their upper arms, shoulders, and back begin to ache. They will soon tire of the activity. A small table and chair will be outgrown from age two to six. Clothes must be replaced as a child grows; so must furniture. Since all five- and six-year-olds are not the same size, classroom furniture should fit different-sized children. If a child is drawing and writing at a kitchen table, a booster chair or stool will raise bent elbows to table height. A stool that is too high is better than one too low.

To develop the thinking skills described earlier, children need access to materials. For example, pattern games, such as sets of large beads, will help to develop *Sequence*. Picture books, especially those that repeat phrases over and over, such as the classic "Gingerbread Boy," will help to develop *Language*. The repeated phrases will encourage the child's participation. Decks of cards that can be used for matching games will help develop *Identicality*.

Children's records or tapes that encourage specific movements to music with a strong rhythm are excellent for building *Directionality* (up-down, front-back, left-right). Fool-proof tape recorders that even the very young can operate independently are also available. Children, of course, enjoy movement activities more if an adult exercises with them, showing them how to listen carefully and follow the instructions and repeating the activity with them several times.

A simple *Equivalence* game can be made from a small collection of varied objects. The child's task is to find two or more items that are "the same" and then tell their common attributes; for example, both are circles, both are red, both are soft, both are for eating. The last task, identifying sameness for a special use, is the hardest to learn. When children have learned this game, the objects can be placed in a sack or "feely box" so children can try to solve the puzzle without visual clues.

If children observe their parents or teachers reading,

they tend to want to learn how to read, too. Similarly, if young children observe adults in meaningful writing activities, they will want to write. Activities like crossing out dates or making special marks on the calendar from day to day help us know what will happen next. This also helps children begin to understand the difficult concepts of *yesterday* and *tomorrow*.

Making a shopping list is an activity in which young children can participate. Before they can write *potatoes* or *raisins*, they can draw these items, and then take the paper to the store to remember what to buy. Gradually, as they learn letters and their corresponding speech sounds, letters and phonetically spelled words will replace the pictures. Encouraging young children to write thank-you notes or letters to their friends while you do the same will establish early the importance of writing. The special reward, of course, will be receiving an answer in the mail.

When young children graduate to pencils, the first pencils need to be extra soft so they will make marks with little pressure. Most children are naturally farsighted until about age seven. They cannot easily see the gray marks made with standard pencils or even with some school primary pencils. To compensate for this natural immaturity of vision, they often hold the pencil in a firm grip, like a weapon. Then they push the pencil onto the paper with heavy pressure in order to make darker marks that they can easily see. Such writing quickly leads to fatigue. Also, the weapon-like grip is a difficult habit to break when retraining the child to hold the writing tool in a more relaxed fashion.

A triangular, soft plastic gripper slipped onto a pencil will help teach a more relaxed grasp of the tool. It will also help teach the efficient three-finger grip (between the thumb and middle finger with the index finger resting on the top). Full-sized pencils are designed for adults to use. Children's first pencils should be about the length of a crayon.

An area sometimes neglected in American preschools and kindergartens is a drawing center, equipped with soft black crayons and plain paper. A painting area does not substitute for this. Children should be encouraged to spend some time daily in such a center. Gradually they will learn to express thoughts and feelings through scribbling and drawing.

Ideally, an adult will interact with children, asking them

to tell about their drawings and then writing a few words on each child's paper, recording the child's own language. Preschools and kindergartens should have a special place, such as the Whole-Language Author's Chair for sharing drawings and first letters and words. (Young children, when sharing, tend to talk primarily to the person in charge, rather than to the whole group. Adults, therefore, should position themselves at the rear of the group to encourage the child author to practice projecting the voice so that all can hear and participate.)

When children try to copy letters adults have written, their first letter making should be assisted the same way parents assist with tooth brushing. If children are making letters with inefficient sequence of strokes, reversals, or bottom-to-top direction, they should be shown the easier, more efficient way to make the letters. Any demonstration, however, should always be on a different surface than the child's paper. A caring adult would not make marks on a child's drawing. His or her writing deserves the same respect. And any of a child's letter-making attempts should be celebrated.

If, for example, a child's first attempts to make *b* and *d* are not assisted, the child will probably begin both letters with a vertical line. The next task will be to place the curves on opposite sides of these letters. Unfortunately, the concept

for left and right for objects outside the body does not normally develop until age 7 or 8. A younger child cannot see the difference between these two letters and will reverse them. This confusion will later spill over into beginning reading. A few minutes of help, showing that the *d* begins with the curve and *b* begins with the vertical line, will prevent later problems.

The *itl* program introduces the letter *d* as a dog standing on its head. Children remind themselves, "head down, feet in the air," while writing the letter, then drawing the rest of the dog with six simple strokes. The letter *d* is taught early in the program because its speech sound is frequent in English. The letter *b* is less needed for beginning writing, so is postponed until later in the program.

## Teaching Alphabet Letters—When to Start?

Rhoda Kellogg's well-documented, long-term field study has taken the guesswork out of this question. Starting in 1928, Kellogg (1970) collected over a million drawings by young children from both primitive and sophisticated cultures throughout the world. From the study of these drawings she reached four major conclusions:

First, children's early designs are similar in form and balance to those found in caves and other remote areas from prehistoric times.

Second, regardless of culture or place of residence, children's early drawings are very much alike. You cannot tell a young artist's ethnic background or home country from the drawings (Figure 2).

Careful inspection of these drawings led Kellogg and her co-workers to the third, most startling revelation: *All children go through the exact same scribbling stages, each stage more complicated than the others, and each one building on the previous one.*

Just as there is a natural hierarchy of stages in motor development (wriggling, rolling, crawling and creeping, standing, walking, running, hopping, galloping, skipping), Kellogg found a similar hierarchy in young children's drawings (Figure 3).

Kellogg did not assign specific ages to these scribbling stages because of natural human variance. Also, growth from one stage to another is dependent both on nature and on nurture—on maturation, over which parents or teachers have little control, and on encouragement, over which they have much control.

Children at similar levels of maturity will vary widely in scribbling development depending upon environmental factors. For example, children may move through the stages more rapidly if they see parents or siblings writing or drawing; if family members or other caretakers encourage scribbling; if they are supplied with suitable scribbling materials; if their child-care center encourages them to draw, as well as paint, at least once a day; if parents or caregivers show approval of scribbling by talking about it, displaying scribbles on the wall, or placing them in an album or file collection.

On the other hand, scribbling is sometimes discouraged.

Bryan (5) has drawn a humanoid and named it ("That's me."). We now know he has the cognitive and physical development to begin writing lowercase letters.

Parents may refuse to have scribbling materials around because they require supervision; brothers and sisters may scoff at a beginner's work; children may hear the statement "No one in our family has any drawing talent"; adults may make complicated drawings for young children to copy.

Children will use less imagination if they are given coloring books instead of inexpensive plain paper for coloring.

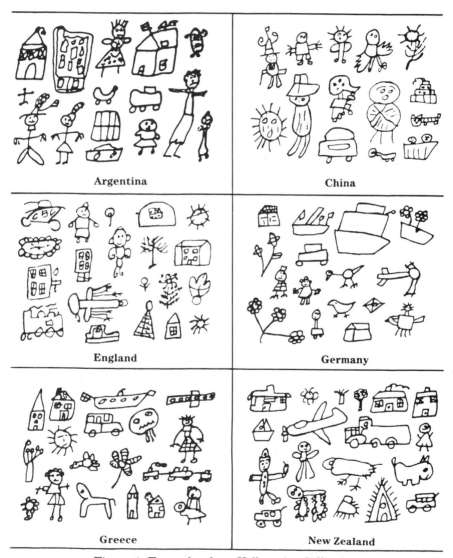

Argentina

China

England

Germany

Greece

New Zealand

Figure 2. Examples from Kellogg Art Collection
(Courtesy of the Golden Gate Kindergarten Association)

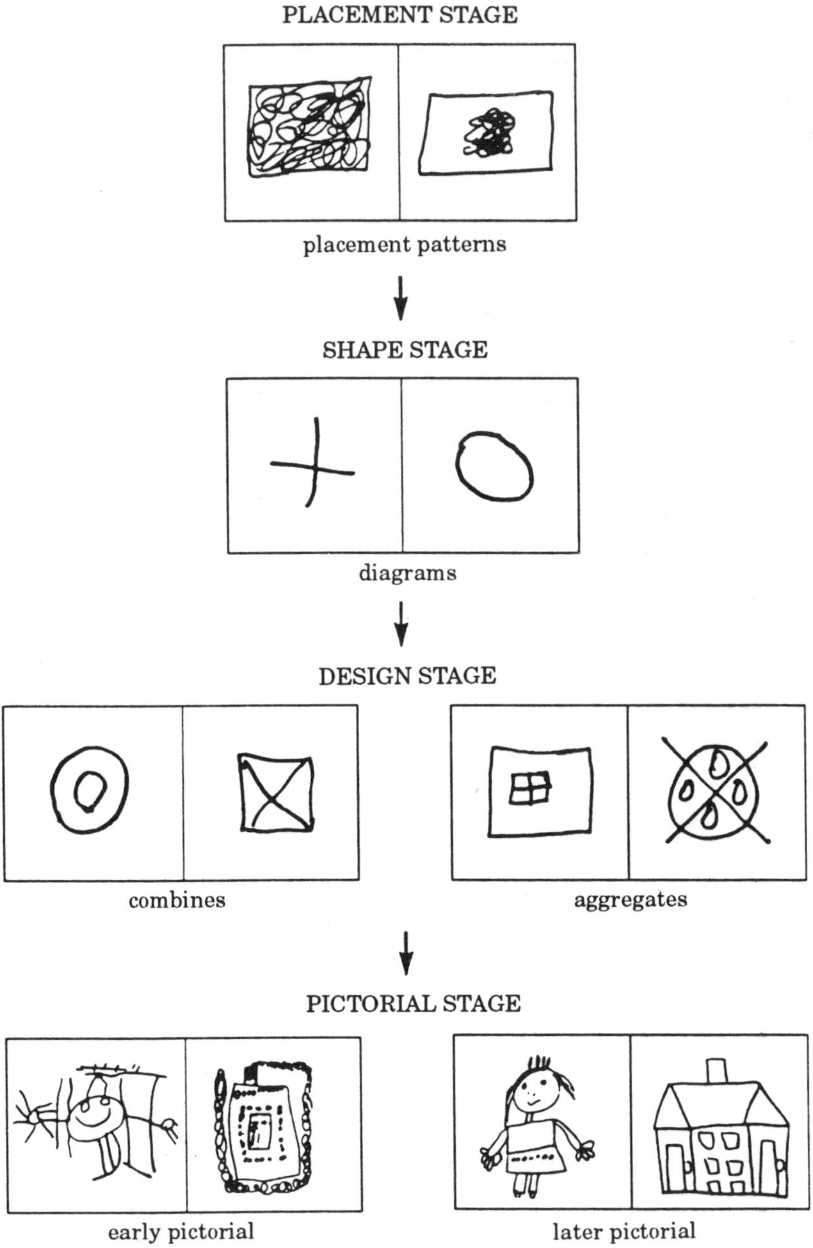

PLACEMENT STAGE

placement patterns

↓

SHAPE STAGE

diagrams

↓

DESIGN STAGE

combines                    aggregates

↓

PICTORIAL STAGE

early pictorial                    later pictorial

Figure 3. Kellogg Drawing Hierarchy
(Courtesy of the Golden Gate Kindergarten Association)

It may discourage children if adults name objects in scribbles, indicating to young children that they should draw something specific instead of simply enjoying their own scribbling designs.

Children whose environments discourage scribbling are more likely to enter school still unready to write.

Kellogg's fourth major conclusion—a child shows obvious readiness to make letters when she or he arrives at Stage 8 or 9 in the Kellogg scribbling hierarchy—clearly answers the question, "When do you start teaching alphabet letters?" When a child has made a closed-line shape with smaller inner circles and rays, she has drawn a primitive human body. At first the rough circle represents the whole body, not just the head. From the small child's viewpoint, looking up at adults, there is little visual differentiation between head and body. The circle is the whole person. Demonstrating to the child that head and body are separate or telling her that arms in the drawing are coming out of the head will only confuse the child; it could set adult standards for drawing that a young child cannot meet. She may stop drawing.

When a child arrives at this stage, it is important to watch and listen but *not* to push or to ask probing questions like "What is that?" or "Is that Mommy?" When the child is ready and voluntarily reports, "That's me!" or "That's Daddy," or in some way gives a name to her person, a major milestone in writing has been reached. Unless the child has copied from another's drawing, or unless someone has helped the child name the drawing, you know three things positively:

- The child has developed the hand-eye coordination to begin to write letters. After all, letters are made up of the same circles and rays as the parts of her primitive person.

- The child has the visual perception needed for writing (making sense out of what she sees). Actually, before children can draw a person, they will often study scribbles and name something seen in a familiar shape. "It's a ball." "It's a tree." These lower-level scribbles, however, are usually unplanned and accidental.

- Most important, when a child names her first hand-drawn person it is an indication that the brain

Spencer can stop his spiral scribble to make a closed-line figure.
"My dad has a mustache."

structures have developed to the point where the child is ready to understand a symbol (something that represents something else). The child has drawn a true symbol and demonstrated a primitive understanding of the thinking skill we call *equivalence.*

While this drawing stage is usually reached around the fourth birthday, a child may draw her first person at age three, age six, or even later for children with mental, emotional, physical, or neurological differences. At that point, regardless of the child's age, the neurological structures controlling both mind and body are ripe and ready to begin to learn to make letters.

You might ask, "Won't this child be more ready if we wait?" Certain areas of the brain develop at specific times of early life (Montessori's "sensitive" periods). If the brain is stimulated through specific experiences at those particular times, the part of the brain that is in a growth spurt will achieve a higher level of efficiency. This is what some learning psychologists refer to as "the match," matching teaching experiences to special stages of development (Hunt, 1961).

The National Association for the Education of Young Children has provided us with a term for Hunt's matching— "Developmentally Appropriate Practice" (Bredekamp, 1987).

There are peak levels of ripeness in fruit. There are peak levels of readiness to learn specifics. The fruit will become overripe if you wait. Children will be less eager to learn to write if you wait beyond the readiness peak.

The illustrations on page 38 show one child's development from scribbling to drawing to writing, and demonstrate the Kellogg hierarchy.

## Children with Special Needs

Standard intelligence tests usually focus on an individual's ability in the areas of language, logic, and numeration. But Howard Gardner, from research with the Project on Human Potential at the Harvard Graduate School of Education (1983), proposes that all of us possess at least seven intelligences. Each person's particular blend of Gardner's seven competences, combining both genetic endowment and cultural expectation, produces a unique cognitive profile. American culture, represented by our schools, stresses the linguistic, logic, and

Sam
11 months
controlled scribble

2 years 1 month
scribbled shapes

3 years
divided shape

3 years 2 months
closed-line shape with rays
on perimeter and eyes

4 years
rays elongated into limbs
Sam has drawn a true symbol.

4 years 9 months
grocery list

mathematical intelligences, but tends to overlook other competences such as the musical, spatial, personal (sensitivity to human needs), and bodily-kinesthetic intelligences.

Certainly no other animal exhibits as much variety in neurological development as humans do. No two human brains have the same connections. We all have unique, individual experiences from the moment of conception. Each of these experiences contributes to the development of our brain. Each of us is just as different on the inside as on the outside. Sometimes these natural differences make it harder to learn the skills of writing and reading.

### Dyslexia

If, for example, a particular brain is organized so that smooth coordination between the right and left hemispheres is harder to achieve, some detours around the blockage need to he learned. Practicing writing (tactile-kinetic input) while at the same time saying the words aloud (auditory-oral input) and then seeing the words written (visual input) has been known to provide detours. This procedure has helped some individuals who are labeled *dyslexic.* That frightening-sounding word simply means "unable to read," or having a "dys" (dysfunction) with "lexic" (words).

According to Piaget (1969), there are levels of symbolizing in young children. First, the two-year-old begins to play-act or pretend. He will, for example, pretend to eat a block and call it a cookie. The second level of symbolizing is drawing. This level leads young children to plan drawings in their heads. The third level is mental imagery. It has been said that dyslexic children seem to lack the ability to make mental images. Such children may have skipped step two in symbolizing development. Encouraging preschoolers to draw is important to developing their ability to make mental images.

I once asked George, a six-year-old, to read a page to me, which he did fluently. George was an adequate decoder. Then I asked him some questions about the content. He was upset with this task. "I read it to you, not to ME! You didn't tell me to listen!" It seems George had not built visual images in his mind while he was reading. He had no memory pictures for recall.

When attempting to remediate older children who are severely reading handicapped, specialists often turn to kinetic methods (writing) when both phonetic- and sight-memory methods have failed. It is possible that by starting with drawing and writing, the disability might have been prevented or lessened. One of the missing links in reading comprehension might be that self-dictation of words—feeling the shape of speech sounds in the mouth while writing the letters in sequence, and simultaneously hearing the noises .and seeing the emerging word designs—develops coordination of the parts of the brain. This coordination is easier to achieve when the language areas of the brain are rapidly maturing, before age five (Koffka, 1959).

A research project by Harvard Medical School, using high-speed computers and sophisticated color graphics, has produced some images of the brain's electrical workings. These new color images have demonstrated a consistent pattern for individuals with major reading disability and those who have been labeled dyslexic. The images show inactivity, not in the brain's visual or auditory centers nor in the interaction between these two major centers usually associated with reading, but in the part of the brain that helps plan complicated motor activity (McKean, 1981).

This research suggests that early drawing and writing activities, both motor based, might stimulate that portion of the brain and prevent or alleviate dyslexia. The motor planning involved in drawing and writing is one of the major basic primary skills to be developed first in the home, in preschools, and as a regular daily period in primary classrooms.

### Learning Disability

The relationship between learning disability and the main steering organ that controls balance and movement, the labyrinth, is discussed by de Quiros (1979). Damage to this part of the inner ear can cause problems with learning tasks requiring movement and spatial orientation. Speaking and writing are movement tasks. Movement of the eyes is also related to reading.

People who advocate getting "back to the basics" in education need to include drawing and movement education as basics. Drawing is the foundation for writing, and writing is one of the foundations for reading.

Recent research (Janet Olson, 1992) reports that children labeled as having a learning disability are often simply *visualizers* rather than *verbalizers*. Most of the world's important inventions were developed by visualizers who first created their designs with mind pictures, then drew them on paper. Edison and Einstein, for example, were visualizers who were not successful in their word-oriented early school environment. Olson recommends that students at all levels draw a story before writing it. The next step is brainstorming a vocabulary list while observing the drawn picture. Finally, students should write the story, using the list as a reference. Drawing is thus the bridge to writing. Such practice, Olson writes, will improve the writing skills of all children, even the more natural verbalizers.

### Gender Differences

Are boys less ready? Isn't it "normal" for girls to learn to write and to read sooner than boys? This is only true in America, where we still revere the "rough and tumble," outdoor male image, or in countries that have copied our educational system. In most of the rest of the world young boys are at least as successful as girls in primary school skills, if not more so. A study of sex differences in reading in four English-speaking nations (Canada, the U.S., England, and Nigeria) found that in grades two through six, girls excelled in Canada and the U.S., and boys excelled in England and Nigeria (Johnson, 1972). A reliable survey of over 1400 research studies of the differences between boys and girls in learning basic academic skills turned up only one major difference. These genetic studies by Maccoby and Jacklin (1974) at Stanford University show evidence of a recessive sex-linked gene that contributes to high spatial ability. Approximately 50 percent of males, but only 25 percent of females show evidence of this inborn factor.

The Denver Developmental Screening Test, used by many pediatricians, indicates that girls seem to have a neurological edge at birth but that boys catch up by their third birthday in personal-social skills, fine-motor/adaptive skills, language and gross-motor skills. Thus, to label boys as less mature at school entrance seems discriminatory (Frankenburg, 1972).

Writing is a spatial act. The Maccoby and Jacklin survey suggests that boys have the innate capacity to learn to write more easily than girls. Yet there are usually more boys than girls in remedial reading groups. This may be because initial instruction for boys in the United States is not through the spatial writing mode, where they have a natural advantage.

### Fine-Muscle Development

Writing is a physical act. Children who are athletic, who have good control of their bodies, will find that writing is easy, provided the instruction is not limited to visual and

Ryan LeTendre (4)

auditory methods. Children who can do a somersault (forward roll) easily can do a roll design (circle or oval) on a surface more easily. Children with physical disabilities, on the other hand, will have to work harder both in movement and in writing.

Sometimes adults use the excuse that particular young children have trouble with writing because they have poor control of the small muscles of the hand. This may be true for older children. Writing for beginners should never be a fine-motor activity, but rather a whole-arm activity. The muscles of the hand and fingers only grasp the writing tool. This is no harder than holding a spoon.

### Handedness
The world's leading authority on handedness (Coren, 1992) writes that "evidence suggests that right-handedness is one of the genetically fixed characteristics associated with being human." It is usually inherited in the same way that the tendency to have five fingers on each hand or the structural characteristics that allow us to walk upright are inherited.

Contrary to common belief, Coren has failed to find any evidence for the inheritance of left-handedness. He contends that the major reason that it tends to occur in families is imitation of family members or other environmental experiences.

On the other hand, ambidextrousness, not having a true lead hand, does seem to be inherited. Somewhere between three and six handedness becomes well established. This trend reflects growth patterns going on in the brain. The two hemispheres of the brain grow at different rates and one gradually establishes its dominance.

Often the infant begins to acquire handedness at the same time that he has a drive to feed himself. If a right-handed parent sits directly in front of the infant at feeding times, the child will tend to grab the spoon with the nearest hand to the spoon, his left. The parent thus inadvertently imprints, or teaches the child to eat with the left hand. The parent then assumes that the child is neurologically left-handed. When that same parent begins to help the child learn to write in the same seated position, the child will naturally reach for the writing tool with the left hand.

If a child has not chosen a lead hand and is not using the same one consistently, writing in a standing position (which is not associated with eating) may be helpful. Often a left-handed eater will turn out to be a right-handed writer. It is easier to learn to write English with the right hand because letters are pulled across the surface from left to right. The left hand, when writing, must learn to push instead, which takes more effort and concentration.

Also, we know that oral language capability is controlled by the left forebrain in all but a small percentage of individuals. This is the same forebrain that controls the right hand. Coordinating the right hand with language is thus an easier task than coordinating the left hand. I once taught a child who ate with the right hand, but wrote with her left hand. Her mother told me that she would not permit her child to eat with the left hand because, "She'd be a social misfit at dinner parties," suggesting that writing is not as important as eating.

One of the early tasks for children learning to write and read is to learn what to attend to and in what order when they look at written language. Clay (1991) tells us that children only need to distinguish between their preferred hand side and the other side. It is not necessary to have developed the verbal concepts for left and right. The *itl* program uses the familiar traffic colors, green and red, to assist beginners in laterality tasks. Green represents GO, or the beginning of a word or a line of print. Red represents STOP, or the end. For introduction of letter orientation, those letters that curve toward the left side are colored green; those curving toward the right side are colored red. Clay also says that the child who writes a few letters usually gains control of left-to right-sequencing before his or her approach to print on a book page. She recommends that directional skills (left to right and top to bottom on a page) be given high priority for beginners, especially in whole-language programs.

### Children with Midline Difficulty

When infants begin to experiment with movement, they relate all movement to the vertical center of the body (midline). Moving the arms from the outside in involves going from left to right for the left arm, and from right to left for the right arm. Later, when the child begins to cross the midline, confusion sets in. The right arm, then on the opposite side of the body, requires a different set of neurological controls. Because of this confusion, some young children tend to avoid activities that require crossing the midline. This avoidance carries over to visual activities that require crossing the midline with the eyes. This will affect writing and reading activities (Lerch, 1974).

Children who avoid crossing the midline are usually right-handed and tend to be perfectionists. They avoid drawing horizontal lines by turning the paper and drawing those lines toward the body.

Exercises that require the crossover of arms and legs may help these children. Standing and drawing horizontal lines at a chalkboard will also help. Some children may move their bodies to avoid crossing over the midline. Taping their paper to a desktop until remediation is complete may force them to draw horizontal lines correctly. Children who consistently make letter reversals are often those who have midline difficulty.

### Deaf or Blind Children

Deaf or hearing impaired children have great difficulty making themselves understood orally. Certainly learning to draw and write should give such children a way to express their innermost feelings. Blind children who have learned sound-symbol correspondence through tactile experience, using the cartoon letter animals of the *itl Integrated Total Language Program*, learn Braille about a year-and-a-half sooner than normally expected. Apparently, learning one symbol system makes it easier to learn a second one.

### Non-English-Speaking Children

For children whose first language is not English, writing would seem to be a suitable activity for both home and school. Writing words, sound by sound, in any language, tends to develop auditory sequencing, as well as the visual discrimination necessary, for later reading. The *itl Integrated Total Language Program* is adaptable to instruction in any language. The animals can be called by any familiar names in the child's native tongue. Having the letters match the beginning sounds of the animals' names is not necessary for success. The child only needs to learn each animal's characteristic noise, such as the mosquito's hum: /mmm/. If a mosquito has a different name in the child's native language, it still makes the same sound and will match the illustrations used in the program. This system has been used to teach Mandarin-speaking children in San Francisco, Spanish-speaking children in the Southwest, and Laotian children in California.

An interesting study in New Zealand (Clay, 1991) compared the school progress of two minority groups, Maori and Samoan. Maori children entered school with a higher level of oral English than the Samoan children. The Samoans, however, scored higher on reading tests both at age six and seven than the Maoris. It was observed that young Samoan children often saw adults writing letters back home to Samoa. Also, the children saw adults reading interesting information received in the mail from these far distant friends and relatives. This was not so common among the Maori families. Apparently the Samoan children learned early the need for writing as communication and realized the value of learning how to do it.

### Autistic Children

My experience with autistic children is limited to just one. This boy had no speaking vocabulary when he was mainstreamed into kindergarten, except that he could recite the alphabet and count to ten. When introduced to the *Integrated Total Language* program, he quickly learned to repeat the single noises of the letter-animals and combine them into meaningful words. Along with this speech development, he drew pictures of the characters and then wrote independent messages. Finally, as Montessori suggested, the child exploded spontaneously into reading with no formal or traditional instruction. Even more important, this boy, though he still has signs of his autism, has voluntarily shared his new skills by teaching other children to write and read.

## Which Modality Should Be Stimulated First?

Making beginning writing and reading as multisensory as possible, rather than restricting the first exercises to visual and auditory presentations, will let children choose and activate the senses that work most efficiently for them. It will also tend to activate the senses that are not naturally coming into play.

A breakthrough at the University of California (Olds, 1975) gives us definite insight into the importance of a specific sensory sequence in the learning process. The brains of laboratory rats were wired, and electronic responses were recorded as each of several skills was learned by the rats. The most primitive areas of the rats' brains gave off electrical signals to indicate their active involvement in the beginning steps of learning. Then other areas of the brain gave off signals as they were activated in the learning process in sequence. Finally, the skill was learned by the higher brain centers. Olds, who was recommended for a Nobel prize for this discovery, worked with the brains of rats because they are miniature versions of human brains.

Applying this theory to human learning, it makes sense to begin stimulation activities with the oldest, most efficient symbolizing sense, then work toward the less developed, higher centers. The *auditory* areas begin to develop shortly after conception (Thomas, 1968). The labyrinth of the inner ear is one of the first parts to develop. Hearing is thus a newborn's most mature sense. A healthy infant soon learns to associate its mother's voice with the expectation of being fed. This is the beginning of associating sound with meaning. The sound is a symbol of the food. It stands for something. This is a low-level cognitive skill. A dog or cat makes this kind of association when the animal expects to be fed at the sound of the can opener.

Using its fully developed hearing sense, the newborn learns easily to control the air passages and mouth parts to produce noises, beginning with the first birth cry. By the end of the first month, a baby can vary the length, pitch, and volume of crying to communicate with others whether she is hungry, wet, tired, or in pain. The second form of symbolizing to develop is *oral*. By the third month, the average infant has figured out that some of the noises she hears are coming out of her own head. This newfound control leads to making more meaningful vocal noises.

In the first few months, an infant will learn to reach out and grab for an interesting object that is hung overhead or a rattle that is held close by. When she is sitting well by herself, at about six months, she will have more opportunities to deliberately reach out and pick up objects. Through these activities, using the nerves at her skin's surface, she learns to discriminate objects by touch, without seeing them. This is also the time the infant recognizes her own special blanket or soft toy. It is the beginning of *tactile* symbolizing.

The part of the brain responsible for coordination of movement makes its most rapid growth between six and fifteen months. This is the period when children learn to sit, crawl, creep, stand, and walk. This is also the time for development of *kinetic* symbolizing—body language. At this time, an infant will usually respond to language with physical movement, as in "patty-cake" or "bye-bye" games. The infant will also respond physically to oral cues. This indicates that there are stronger connections developing in the brain between the auditory and kinetic areas. Soon the child will initiate kinetic symbolizing independently, raising the arms, for example, to indicate a need to be picked up.

At birth, the child's eyes have not yet learned to work together. It is dark in the womb and the eyes have not had the practice needed to develop vision. Infants do, however, respond to light and are able to fix their gaze on definite dark and light patterns from the beginning of life outside the womb. Recognition of, and responding to such *visual* symbols as pictures, however, does not usually occur until sometime between the eighth and eleventh month. It takes about the same length of time for visual perception to develop in adults who are blind from birth and receive the gift of sight through today's miraculous surgery.

In summary, a symbol is something that represents something else. The parts of the human brain that control symbolizing develop from birth roughly in this sequence: *auditory, oral, tactile, kinetic,* and *visual.* This inward development is evident in outward activities observed during the first year of life after birth.

In Kaufman's report (1977) of his family's remarkable rehabilitation of their son, who was diagnosed at two years with incurable infantile autism, the sequence of symbolizing hierarchy can be traced. First the little boy responded to sound. Next he began to make meaningful squeals and grunts. Tactile and kinetic symbolizing followed with manipulation of toys and body language. Understanding two-dimensional pictures came last.

The *itl Integrated Total Language Program* capitalizes on this natural symbolizing development. First the adult reads a story in which the child hears an animal noise, such as the mosquito's hum, "mmmmm." Next, the child is encouraged to repeat the same noise. Then the adult needs to make the child aware of how her mouth and throat feel when she says the sound. The child then needs to become kinetically involved with movement activities related to the particular noise, such as drawing the letter, showing the signing symbol for the hearing impaired, and or pretending to be the animal that makes the noise. Finally, teaching should include activities in which the child recognizes the letter alone.

With practice, most children will be able to reverse the sequence and eventually respond with any of the five modes when presented with any of the other modes. When children can close the circle, from visual to auditory, or reverse the operation (skipping the kinetic-tactile stages), they will have acquired the decoding and encoding foundation skills for beginning writing and reading.

Most phonics programs suggest that teachers begin by showing letters to children (visual input), then trying to teach the related speech sounds (auditory input). This is the reverse of natural development. We should instead begin with the known—the speech sounds in the children's language repertoire—then work toward the unknown—the letters representing those sounds.

### Perceptual Differences

*Perception* implies understanding of what you have perceived sensually—a higher level of thinking than simply receiving the sensory input. Young, physically healthy children have more strength in auditory perception than in visual perception. David, for example, will correct you if you call him "Bavid." He can do this long before he can tell you that the letters *b* and *d* face in different directions, a visual-spatial task. On the other hand, young children have more strength in visual memory than in auditory memory. It is easier to remember faces than names. A strong symbolizing program should capitalize on these two strengths: *auditory* perception, but visual *memory*. The *itl Integrated Total Language Program* starts with a particular sound, then builds memory traces around the sound with picture symbols to build visual memory.

Some philosophers and psychologists tell us that for inner peace, all life should be in balance (yin/yang). In the early experiences of our American youngsters we possibly build tension by bombarding their senses with too much receptive experience without a similar amount of expressive experience for balance. Television, for example, is a totally receptive activity. So are many school reading lessons. We need to encourage more expressive activities such as singing, dancing, drawing, and writing.

Writing for beginners does not need to be a sedentary act. Drawing letters with brush and water on a wall or warm sidewalk is a satisfying activity (and all errors magically disappear). Writing at an easel will encourage large, clear letters made with the whole arm instead of scrawled with tight fingers. Children enjoy curling their bodies into letters they know. Groups of children can thus dance into words. All of these activities can be adapted to all young children, even those with physical, emotional, mental, or neurological differences.

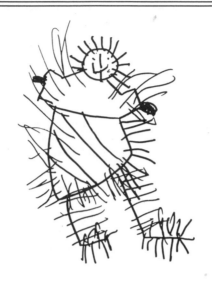

I am the
ubominubl
shoman.

*Part 2*

# GUIDING CHILDREN'S EARLY WRITING EXPERIENCES

## *Original Composition*

Two false attitudes dominate American culture today:

- Reading is the key to all later learning.
- Writing is a special art, a talent possessed by a gifted few.

All children can write if we show them how. How does one lead young children from letters to syllables, to words and sentences, and finally to paragraphs?

Professionals sometimes recommend a method called *language experience*. This method purports to teach the child that

anything I think, I can say;
anything I say, I can write;
anything I write, I can read;
anything I write can also be read and understood
by someone else.

Some language-experience programs skip over completely or only lightly touch on the relationship of letters to their most common speech sounds. Some begin abruptly by expecting beginners to write and spell words that have difficult deviant spelling patterns such as the outlaw words in Appendix C.

Early experiences with written language should show children that written language is a system. We do not begin math instruction by teaching young children to memorize or copy number combinations before showing them that math is a system. We begin, instead, by showing children that each individual number has a specific value. We put them together in different combinations to get different quantities. Why not do the same with written language instruction?

Some language programs begin by having adults do the writing for students as students dictate. Sometimes these are group efforts in which selected children dictate parts of a short story. The purpose, of course, is to demonstrate to children that written words are pictures of spoken words. Certainly this practice has value for groups of preschoolers or immature, kindergarten groups. We need, however, to be aware of some of the possible problems.

For example, does the adult write exactly what the child says so that the child sees a direct translation of his or her own words? If the child says, "Him gots a ball," or "I be in the park," the adult most likely edits the child's words into school-correct language and writes, "He has a ball," and "I am in the park." If the child then reads these words back into their original form, the ones he actually said, does this help him understand the relationship between speech, writing, and reading? Or does it just help the child remember and guess? Does this activity build the child's self-esteem, or does it possibly confirm the conviction that writing is too difficult for him to do alone, and that he can only copy? Correct usage can be taught through verbal modeling and by reading to children, but not as part of beginning writing.

Problems may arise if aides who write the children's words are not trained for this activity. They may not form alphabet letters correctly or in the correct stroke sequence, thus demonstrating the skill incorrectly.

If copying the words is the expected follow-up, children need to be observed closely so that they are immediately shown how to form any letters that they make with inefficient or reversed stroke sequences. Another danger is that young children may be expected to copy from a chart story on the wall, alternating with each letter from far-point to near-point vision. This causes severe eye-muscle strain. Worse yet, young children may be expected to copy from a chalkboard, changing from white letters on a dark ground to dark letters on a light paper.

The major difficulty with most Language Experience programs for beginners is that they start with twenty-six alphabet letters in both lower- and upper-case forms, representing forty-four sounds of language.

Teaching young children to write as we teach them to talk—slowly, step by step, sound to syllable, to word, to sentence, to paragraph—is a far better approach than starting with the sentence and reversing the order. Also, the child who is taught to write from eye to hand develops different brain paths from one whose memory is tracked from mouth to ear to hand to eye (Reimer, 1969). A writer is first a talker. He feels words. He feels his mouth and lips forming them. He feels whether his lips are relaxed or tightened, whether his tongue is touching his teeth or up on the roof of his mouth, and whether his larynx is activated or not. The beginning writer needs to feel differences in his mouth and throat as he forms spoken words. The beginning writer writes the letters in sequence for the sounds that he *feels* and *hears* himself make. Copying words written by another person (either one's own words or someone else's words written down by another person) mistrains the brain by reversing the writing process. The neurological process that the child must develop is speech—to ear—to hand—to eye. Shortcuts or detours will only slow down the necessary development of brain paths for writing.

Following is a step-by-step procedure for developing the necessary neurological pathways to writing:

1. As soon as a child learns to write a single vowel and a consonant, then you can begin dictation by blending the sounds into a syllable.

2. Dictate the two sounds slowly in sequence.

3. Ask the child to repeat the syllable aloud and to write the two letters representing the speech sounds in correct left-to-right pattern. If errors are made, the child should cross out and write the letters again but not erase.

4. Have the child run her or his fingers under the syllable, left to right, and repeat it aloud.

This is the speech—to ear—to hand—to eye process. The child needs to learn to say it, feel it, hear it, write it, read it.

The *itl Integrated Total Language Program* introduces the letters *i* and *t* first and then blends these into the word *it*. Then children play a game to stimulate comprehension in which someone is "it." The first sentence dictated—*it lit*—uses only three letters. Capital letters are not taught at this point. Children are taught to space between words and use a period as a "stop sign." Children are then led to illustrate their own writing with original interpretations. Various pictures emerge, such as a lighted match, a bonfire, a lamp, or even a bug, a bird, or a plane coming in for a landing.

Daily drawing with a black, soft crayon or felt-tipped pen is important for developing both the visual-motor integration for letter writing, and also for developing the visual imagery so necessary for composition and for later reading comprehension and enjoyment. Adults should encourage children to elaborate their drawings by asking questions such as, "Who else was there?" or "What was in this big space over here?" When children indicate that their black-on-white pictures are complete, then they can be encouraged to use other crayons to color the picture.

Following the first dictated sentence, regular, frequent dictation continues with words and sentences following the simplest phonetic patterns of English. (See Appendix A.) Children do not worry about spelling because no words with irregular patterns are used. Holding up a finger for each letter while dictating helps children get all the letters in and helps them self-check. This is especially important with words ending in a blend of two consonants. such as *left* or *went*. Without seeing a finger for each sound, children are likely to write *let* and *wet*.

Experiences with the field testing of the *itl Integrated Total Language Program* indicate that it takes about a year to cover the entire lowercase alphabet using this process with a group of four-year-olds. The average kindergarten class can do it in less time. Certainly not all children will master writing all letters by sound in that time.

Whether or not they are mature enough to do any letter writing, all children can enjoy hearing the *itl* stories about the letter-animals who make funny noises. And all children can draw pictures about the stories. The program is thus developmentally appropriate for the natural differences in young children.

A chart of letters with picture references should be posted where children can see it. The alphabet dictation exercises described here can be done successfully by a parent at home or with groups of children in a school setting.

Once the basic sound-symbol system has been learned, it is time to begin step two, independent composition, or self-dictation. The most productive time for composition with school groups is on a Monday, when most of the students have had different experiences over a weekend. This activity should begin with a very small group. Teachers who are learning how to teach original composition should probably start with not more than two children at a time. It is not necessary that all children begin independent writing the same week, or the same month. The rest of the class can be engaged in other quiet, independent activities. Both thinking and writing are impossible to achieve when other children are engaged in noisy block play, chasing each other, replaying a TV show of the night before, or riding tricycles around the writing table. Other children should be encouraged to use "inside voices" at this time so as not to disturb the writers.

Give each child in the writing group a paper and a soft black crayon. Ask children to close their eyes. Children who cannot keep their eyes closed can hold their hands over their eyes. The game is to "make pictures in your head." Ask the children to think about some activity that took place during their own weekend. It can be a pleasant event or a disaster. It can be as simple as eating a meal or going to bed. Try to promote visual imagery by asking questions such as

Were you inside or outside?

Who was with you?

Can you remember what you were wearing?

What kind of furniture was in the room?

Tell children not to answer the questions—their pictures will tell the answers. While their eyes are still closed, say: "When I tell you to open your eyes, draw the picture that is in your head. Start by drawing yourself into the picture. Then draw what was around you. Ready, now open your eyes and begin."

If children have been drawing every day while learning the lowercase alphabet and its related speech sounds, they will have no difficulty drawing. While the children are finishing their pictures, you are free to engage each child in conversation about the event the child is drawing. From this interchange you can select a simple sentence that will be fairly easy for the child to write. For some children writing a single word or phrase will be enough to start; dictate the words to the child very slowly, sound by sound. If a child has forgotten a letter or sound, use the wall chart for reference. Remind children where to put spaces between words and where to put the period. Each child must first say the word slowly, then write each letter in sequence.

Gradually, over a period of weeks, some children will graduate to completely independent writing. They will no longer need an adult to repeat their words. They will have learned to listen carefully to their own speech. These same activities can be done at home. Parents and teachers must, however, be ready to accept children's first invented spelling. Pulaski (1971) quotes Piaget, "Children have real understanding only of what they invent themselves. Each time we try to teach them something too quickly, we keep them from re-inventing it themselves."

From this process, such delightful stories emerge as this one, shared by Carol Chomsky (1975), a specialist in children's early language:

"The ckoral snack is a ciend of radoler. The spiting koebera is won of the sdrogist snacks. And the gient ckobera is the sdrogist!"

Translation: *The coral snake is a kind of rattler. The spitting cobra is one of the strongest snakes. And the giant cobra is the strongest!*

This youngster has obviously learned the two-letter blend *ck,* but he does not yet know that it is not used at the beginning of English words. He knows that an *e* is added to help a vowel say its alphabet name (*ciend*). He is practicing what he knows. Typically at this level some letters are left out of consonant groups (*sdrog* for *strong*). Voiced and unvoiced consonant pairs are interchanged (*t-d*). The difficult "outlaw" word *one* has not yet been memorized. However, these first compositions can be decoded, with practice, by reading them aloud.

Won't invented spelling continue as a lifelong bad habit? It will if you don't lead the child from step one to the next step. Spelling, like speech, is taught gradually. (See spelling levels on page 98.)

Karina and Veronica have communicated clearly
using invented spelling.

Andrea and Duane have written the
sounds they hear in *was*.

It is interesting to observe the gradual self-correction of such outlaw words as *saw*, *the*, and *was*. *Saw* usually appears in first compositions as *so*. The beginning inventive speller uses the *o* that he knows in *off*. When the child discovers the word *saw* in first reading lessons, the *w* then appears on the end of the word. *Saw* becomes *sow*. The vowel does not change to *a* until later. *Was* follows a similar spelling development. The ending first changes from *wuz* to *wus*. The vowel changes last. *The* appears first as *thu*, using the known vowel, *u* as in *up*. This word changes quickly to *the* as reading begins.

Once young children have invented their own spelling system, adapting basic alphabetic writing to their own spoken language, they are ready to deal with the difficult conventional spellings of English in reading and writing. A follow-up of my own long-term field study shows that children who are encouraged to write with invented spelling in kindergarten and first grade and then are taught basic spelling rules and the outlaw words test at a higher level by fifth grade in both spelling and reading than children who are taught dictionary spelling first (Connell, 1975).

At the very beginning, children's writings are usually only recordings of personal events. After a substantial amount of this journal-type practice, children are ready to branch out into fiction or imaginary stories. Nonfiction comes first.

The following group of compositions by kindergarten children, done near the end of the school year, are typical of beginning journal writing after children have been taught letter formation and sound-symbol correspondence.

These children could write, but they could not read, not even their own stories. Reading did follow, however, after several weeks of independent writing.

Gradually, children learn through writing to express feelings, both conscious and unconscious. Writers, like artists, often do not know what they want to express until the task is finished. At times we do not understand our own feelings until we put them down on paper. Writing becomes therapy. Home and school can contribute to better communication and better mental health by encouraging young children to write.

Kirsten P.
me and my famly had brecfast
estr morning.

Kirsten P.

AnneMarie
Mi cat is going to hav kitens.

Anne Marie

Nonie

Elena

Susannah

Ryan

Cameron

DUtch and I Practist socr and tenis.

Cameron's drawn people stand on a ground line, showing
readiness to read in a left-right pattern.

Greg
We Went to thu ucwer eum.

We so u scwid.

Greg has sounded out *aquarium*.

## Phonics

In teaching reading, there are many different opinions about where to start. Is it best to tell children the traditional names of the letters, to tell them the equivalent speech-sound values, or both?

It is possible that we are on the wrong track when we postpone teaching children the sound values of letters on the premise that this skill is more difficult to learn than alphabet letter names. A toddler usually attempts to say, "woof woof," before he says, "dog." Something approximating "meow" comes before "kitty," and "moooo" is said before "cow." Animal sounds seem to occur before names of animals. Recently I observed a youngster closely watching a panting dog. The child was not quite one year old. Spontaneously, he imitated the dog: /h h h h/. The next day the child was looking at a picture book with his mother. When he saw a picture of a dog, without prompting, he began to pant /h h h h/. He was not ready to name the animal, but he was ready to associate a sound with it.

Children in this country are bombarded on all sides by letters and other symbols—on packages, on television, in magazines, newspapers, and children's books, even on their containers of disposable diapers—from the moment of birth. There is no way to escape from this barrage of letters. It is only natural that, as soon as the child can communicate effectively, he will begin to point to letters and ask, "What's dat?"

Parents listen carefully for their infant's first attempts to make single speech noises and then gradually to blend them into syllables, nonsense words, meaningful words, and finally sentences. At each step along the way parents respond to the child, repeating his noises, making other noises, and encouraging the child to continue in the learning process by showing obvious pleasure at his accomplishment.

Infants begin to combine the voice noises they know into syllables and repeated syllables sometime before their first birthday (mama, papa, dada, tata, wawa, baba). At first they are just making noises for their own auditory entertainment. Parents and caregivers attach and teach the meanings.

The tasks of learning to talk and learning to write are similar; each task has about the same sequence of steps and each one takes about two years for the average child to master—that is, to go from single noises or letters to simple sentences. The English language is made up of about thirty-eight to forty-four single speech sounds, depending upon dialect, regional pronunciation, place of residence, and the speech patterns of one's own parents.

Communicating in written language requires learning to write forty-four different letter symbols representing the various speech sounds of English (twenty-six lowercase letters and eighteen capital letters). Eight letters can be made identically in both upper- and lowercase *(C, O, S, U, V, W, Y,* and *Z).*

As soon as young children learn to write a few letters, they can begin to learn to combine them into easy, regularly spelled words—a far more interesting activity than learning the entire alphabet in isolation.

Some time ago, when my youngest son was not quite four, he climbed into my lap and pointed to a large S in the headlines of the newspaper I was reading. Mike asked, "What's dat?" I had had no professional teaching courses or experience at that time. I answered simply, "It looks something like a snake, doesn't it? Snakes say SSSSSSSS." I was not trying to prematurely stuff phonics into my child, just giving an honest answer to a sincere question. Later that same day, Mike dragged the newspaper to me, pointed to a letter *s* in the smallest print, and said, "This one's only a worm. What does a worm say?"

That evening Mike announced to me excitedly, "l know your secret! I know why letters are pictures of noises you say. It's because they're animals! The animals are invisible but we can see their skeletons. Letters are animal skeletons. The invisible animals make noises. That's how you read and write, isn't it?"

In the months that followed, Mike would select a letter, write it carefully, then ask for its special noise in the language. He would think about it for a while, then choose an animal with this particular "skeleton." He would then proceed to primitively cartoon the animal around the letter. Next he would make up a story, telling why the animal made that particular noise. Last he would add a comic-book-style "talking balloon" and fill it with the same letter to show the noise the animal was making in the story.

His letter *t* turned into a turtle who had mislaid her

I am in Camoflosh

Cloz so the dyr

wont sy my. I looc

lic the boosh Us

Andrew (4 1/2) uses the letter *y* for the /ee/ sound, which
he knows at the end of *mommy* and *daddy*.

watch but could hear it ticking /t t t/. She had absent-mind-
edly hung the watch around her neck! Mike thought it was
hilarious that she couldn't find it. My role in Mike's letter
game was simply to supply him with the major speech sound
in English represented by each letter he selected, help him
make the letters correctly, listen to his stories, and admire
his drawings.

Mike's self-imposed phonic play, turning letters into

imaginary animals, was no more difficult for him than pointing to animals in picture books and saying their noises: "The cow says MOOOOO." By the time he entered kindergarten, Mike had taught himself to write and to read through his letter games. Mike's invented system for learning sound-symbol correspondence became the *itl Integrated Total Language Program.*

### Why Not Start with Traditional Alphabet Names?

Learning traditional alphabet names for letters doesn't teach children what they need to know to write independently. Remedial reading classes are full of students who can tell you letter names, but are unable to use letters. Letters are simple outline designs we use to represent speech sounds. Until we learn which letters represent specific speech sounds, we will be unable to write independently, except for a limited number of memorized words.

Some teachers say it is *harder* to teach the "sounds" than the "names" of letters. Is it harder to remember /es/ or to remember /ssss/? /em/ or /mmmm/? /vee/ or /vvvv/? Another reason given for teaching names first is that often the child doesn't hear the sounds or "has poor auditory perception." However, I believe that a child who can hear *two* sounds—the vowel and the consonant sound in the alphabet name— should certainly be able to hear the one speech sound represented by the same letter. For a teacher who has not had instruction in phonics, or in how to teach phonics, it may *seem* easier to teach alphabet names—especially since many children have already learned the names prior to school entrance.

Certainly, learning the names of alphabet letters is important. However, it is step two in teaching literacy, *not* step one. The letters *a, e, i, o, u,* for example, do sometimes represent their alphabet names in written words (*ape, eat, ice, over, use*). These five alphabet letter names must eventually be learned. But these letters represent their alphabet name sounds only about 20 percent of the time in written English. The short-vowel sounds (*at, edge, in, on, under*) still make up most of our daily language (Dewey, 1970).

Also, the long-vowel sounds (alphabet names) are much harder to apply to written language because of their complicated spelling patterns. Most of the time when one writes words with long-vowel sounds, extra cues, such as silent letters, are needed to indicate the long-vowel sound. While these "silent" letter cues are important, they are difficult for beginners. These letter-name sounds can be taught after the more frequent, short-vowel sounds are being used in beginning writing.

If young children already know alphabet names, are they handicapped by this knowledge? When two similar or related things are taught in a relatively short time (left and right, for example), this sometimes leads to confusion. Alphabet names are simply not so important. Children will need to use them less frequently in learning to write and to read. It is far easier to teach the major sounds for letters to young children who have not learned the alphabet names for letters. The solution suggested in the *itl Integrated Total Language Program*, if children already know letter names, is to explain that they have already learned the "last" names for these letters, or their "family names," and that now they will learn the most-used "first" names. Children already know the last names of some of their friends and relatives and know that the first names are used more often.

### Teaching Beginning Sounds

One of the common reading-readiness activities in American schools is teaching beginners to isolate the beginning speech sounds of whole words. For generations, this has been the focus of alphabet books. (*B* is for *ball*.) Schoolchildren who are not successful in these tasks are sometimes labeled "unready" for reading, or "weak in auditory sequencing." These same children could probably tell you that ball ends with /lll/ and that it rhymes with *fall*. What is heard last is easier to recall. Listen to two-year-olds repeating the names of animals in a picture book. Commonly you hear /awgy/, not /daw/, for *dog*. You will hear /raf/ for *giraffe*. Rhyming—matching the last syllables of words—is a more suitable exercise for very young children than learning beginning sounds of words.

Phonics can be taught to kindergarten-age and even younger children, but the methods and activities must be suitable for this period of development. A watered-down first-grade program, in which children are expected to know the beginning sounds of words, will only cause frustration for a substantial portion of kindergarten-age children. The *itl*

*Integrated Total Language Program* is successful with young children because it fits the learning style of most young children. It stresses learning through the kinetic mode. Young children learn best by doing, not by looking, listening, or memorizing.

Concerned parents sometimes purchase workbooks for five-year-olds that have been designed for seven-year-olds. Usually these books expect children to associate letters with their speech sounds. This is a very difficult task if children have not played a number of sound games and learned to listen carefully and isolate speech sounds. Phonics can be taught to four- and five-year-olds, but not with workbooks.

The Phonics Guide on page 71 is nontraditional but functional. The beginning-sound concept is avoided as much as possible to simplify the task. When teaching sounds to children, it is important to remember not to add a voiced /uh/ at the end of isolated consonant speech sounds. For example, hum *m* /mmmm/; don't say /muh/. This error in pronunciation is more likely to occur in making beginning word sounds because they are followed by vowel sounds. It is harder, for example, to isolate the sound at the beginning of the word dog than the sound at the end of the word. When saying the sounds in *dog*, people are more likely to say /duh/ than /guh/, because the *g* in *dog* is not followed by a vowel sound.

The speech sounds for the letters *w, y,* and *qu* are not followed by an /uh/. These letters should not be pronounced as /wuh/, /eeuh/, and /coo-uh/. We do not say /wuh-et/ for *wet*, /ee-uh-es/ for *yes*, or /coo-uh-ick/ for *quick*.

A few speech sounds or letters do not regularly appear at the end of English words, so a beginning sound or letter has been used instead. Also, vowel sounds are more easily isolated in the beginning of syllables or words.

Looking in a mirror to watch the position of the mouth parts when making a particular sound helps, especially if you cannot hear the difference between similar sounds (as in the short *i* and *e* in *pin* and *pen*). Looking at your face while making sounds will help *show* the difference. Feel the difference first by looking, and then with your eyes closed.

There are basically two kinds of speech sounds—vowels and consonants. Vowels are made by varying the opening at the top of the larynx, like stretching the neck of a balloon full of air. When the neck of the larynx is fully stretched, it is prepared for making the high-pitched sound /ee/. When it is relaxed, the larynx is prepared for making the sound at the beginning of *up*. All thirteen American-English vowel sounds can be made by changing the shape of the mouth to vary the size of the cavity and the mouth opening.

Short vowels are called *short* because we make only one sound when we pronounce them (*a*t, *e*dge, *i*n, *o*n, *u*nder). Long vowels are sometimes referred to by linguists as *diphthongs* because four of these sounds are made by blending two vowel sounds together. Look in your mirror. You can see and feel your mouth take two different positions when you pronounce *a* as in the word *make*. The long sound for this letter, *a*, starts out like the *e* in *edge*, then glides into /ee/. What we call "long i" starts out as /ah/, then glides into /ee/. Long *o* begins with the mouth in a middle-sized position, then shrinks into /oo/. Long *u* begins with /ee/, then glides to /oo/. That is why these vowels are called long. Two sounds are simply longer to the ear than one. The long *e* is the exception. The mouth does not change position when making this sound.

The letters in the Phonics Guide are divided into groups according to their writing difficulty. The cue word is written to be read and said aloud, listening carefully for the italicized letter sound. Spelling the word aloud using letter names will not isolate the American-English speech sound.

## Phonics Guide

### Easy Sounds

| | | | |
|---|---|---|---|
| /i/ | in | /u/ | up |
| /t/ | cat | /r/ | or |
| /l/ | bell | /n/ | in |
| | | /h/ | hot |
| /j/ | edge | /m/ | him |
| /c/ | music | /p/ | up |
| /a/ | at | /b/ | cab |
| /d/ | sad | | |
| /f/ | if | /w/ | new |
| /g/ | dog | /y/ | happy |
| /o/ | on | /k/ | make[2] |
| /s/ | bus | /v/ | have |
| /s/ | is[1] | /x/ | box |
| /e/ | edge | /z/ | buzz[3] |

### Two-Letter Consonant Sounds

(Digraphs)

| | |
|---|---|
| /qu/ | quick (coo) |
| /th/ | this, bathe[4] |
| | |
| /th/ | bath, thin |
| /ch/ | itch |
| /sh/ | fish |
| /ng/ | song |
| /wh/ | when[5] |

---

1. The letter *s* represents the sound /z/ more often than the letter *z*, so is taught first.
2. The same sound as for the letter *c*.
3. The same as the second sound for the letter *s*.
4. This is the most common sound for *th*, so is taught first.
5. Originally spelled *hw*, because of the beginning blast of air, represented by the letter *h*. This speech sound is gradually disappearing from American English. See the section on spelling.

**Name Sounds of Vowels**

/a/ *a*pe
/e/ *ea*t[1]
/i/ *i*ce
/o/ *o*pen
/u/ *u*se

**Other Vowel Sounds**

/u/ bl*ue* (sometimes spelled *oo* as in t*oo*)
/u/ p*u*t sometimes spelled *oo* as in b*oo*k)
/aw/ *aw*ful[2]

There are only so many ways the body parts that make voice sounds can be combined. This number is doubled by movement of the larynx. The following pairs of consonant sounds are formed identically in the mouth. Some, however, activate the larynx and some do not. The vibrations of the voiced sounds can be felt by placing your fingers lightly on your throat as these sounds are said.

| *Unvoiced* | *Voiced* |
|---|---|
| /p/ | /b/ |
| /c/ | /g/ |
| /t/ | /d/ |
| /f/ | /v/ |
| /s/ | /z/ |
| /th/ (ba*th*) | /th/ (*th*is) |
| /sh/ | /zh/ (vi*si*on) |
| /ch/ | /j/ |
| /x/ | /x/ (e*x*amination) |

---

1. Another way to write the sound taught with the letter *y*.
2. Some American speakers do not distinguish between this speech sound and the common sound for o as in on. Look at your face in the mirror and say *hot dog*. If your mouth looks smaller with the *o* in *dog* than the *o* in *hot*, you normally use both of these speech sounds. Try it with *on* and *off*. Don't try to teach these two vowel sounds if you don't normally use them, or you may confuse children.

## Alphabet Letter Forms

An error commonly made both by laypersons and some professionals is to begin teaching writing with capital letter forms. Sometimes people believe that capital letters are easier to make because they are bigger. Drive on any highway and you can see that it is possible to make any form of letter the size of a barn. Reading the newspaper, you can see that it is possible to make any style of letter as small as a crumb. Size does not make sense as a criterion for teaching the capital letter forms first.

Over two thousand years ago our classical capital letters were developed by the Romans with clean-cut lines, to be carved in stone (Figure 4). No one has ever improved on these designs. They are easy to distinguish from one another and, *when taught correctly*, are rarely reversed. The name *capital* refers to the head (caput) or upper part of a column or pillar of a structure—where these letters were usually carved. Carving in stone required that the letter forms be made of separate strokes for each change of direction.

To learn to reproduce these capital, start-and-stop letters requires constant decisions about direction of the strokes. Young children are usually not ready to make these decisions because their knowledge of left and right is still not completely refined. Some average children are not sure of left and right orientation on objects outside their own body until age eight or later. Some adults have never acquired this skill because of inadequate early instruction.

Capital letters take sixty-four separate strokes or changes of direction to make the full alphabet from *A* to *Z*. Lowercase letters made in the common manuscript form taught in most American schools today require fifty-three changes in direction. Capital letters require twenty diagonal strokes—the most difficult strokes for young children to make. Lowercase letters require only fourteen diagonal strokes.

Children see lowercase letters more frequently because they are used more often. Children's books are usually printed in lowercase letters, the capitals used only as the first letter of names or sentences and, occasionally, titles. Lowercase recognition is much more important to beginning reading.

Figure 4. Roman capitals

### Why Not Teach Upper- and Lowercase Letters at the Same Time?

When both forms are taught simultaneously, young children tend to believe they can be used interchangeably. They tend to write in a hit-or-miss fashion, mixing the two forms. This makes it doubly difficult to teach the rules of capitalization at a later date. WouLD You accePT, PriNTeD MaTTEr in haPhazarD foRm, CApiTaLs aND LoWercasE MixeD? The sooner young children learn to use lowercase letters appropriately, the more legible their writing will become.

Certainly capitals do need to be taught. As soon as lowercase letters are being written comfortably and fluently, children can learn to make capitals. This is also a good time to teach the simplest rules of capitalization (at the beginning of names and sentences and for titles). One exception might be an earlier teaching of the first initial of the child's own name. Do not be surprised, however, if the child finds this task difficult. Capital *A*, for example, is one of the hardest letters to make. It has diagonal strokes going in two different directions, and three exact joinings where the strokes meet. Capital *M* and *W* are even more difficult.

American toy manufacturers and television programs often give equal importance to both capital and lowercase letters. Parents and teachers may have to shop very carefully to find materials using lowercase letters for writing games for young children. Often the products that use lowercase letters are manufactured in Europe.

### Which Lowercase Form Is Best for Beginners?

Alphabet history gives us some clues about which forms of lowercase letters to use with beginners. Roman capitals were used in Europe until around the eighth century. As scribes and calligraphers experimented with different writing tools, such as brushes, quills, and broad-edged reeds, as well as with different writing surfaces, they invented new alphabets to simplify the task. They left out unnecessary parts of capital forms: for example, they simplified *B* to *b*. They made each letter with one continuous line, rather than in separate strokes (Figure 5).

When Charlemagne discovered that each area of his western European empire was developing its own simplified

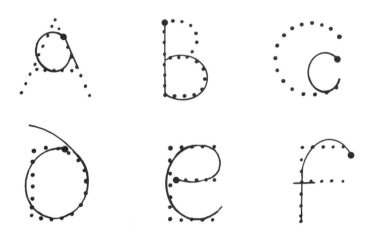

Figure 5. Simplified continuous-line letters
derived from roman capitals

shorthand forms for letters, he realized that this lack of uni-
formity would confuse communication. He imported Alcuin of
York, a monk known for his skill in calligraphy, to design a
common alphabet. Charlemagne then decreed that Alcuin's
alphabet be used throughout his empire, most of the western
European continent. This standardized form of lowercase letters was called the Carolingian alphabet. Areas of Europe not
under Charlemagne's control developed different alphabet
forms, such as modern Greek and Russian.

The Carolingian alphabet was slightly revised during the
Renaissance and called the *humanist book hand*. When the
monks were copying church documents to preserve the origi-
nals, their rapid style of writing became more slanted, circles
changing to ellipses. This church-related style was referred to
as *chancery cursive* (Figure 6).

Venetian scribes in the fifteenth century made slight
changes in *chancery cursive*. They put flat tops on some letters in which the first stroke was toward the left. We use this
more slanted form of lowercase letters for special emphasis
today and call it *italic*.

The baroque period added ruffles, flourishes, fancy deco-
rations, and swirls. At this time swing strokes were added so
that all letters in each word were joined together.

In colonial America these baroque forms were simplified
to be used for engraving; the simplified forms were called

Figure 6. Chancery cursive lowercase alphabet

*roundhand* or *copper plate*. In the nineteenth century, publishers of handwriting materials removed more of the flourishes, but kept the joining strokes (Figure 7). They also kept the fancy baroque capitals, eleven of which are completely different from roman capitals (Figure 8). This is the form of cursive writing usually taught in American schools today, beginning about the third grade. When drawn slowly it is an art form. When written quickly it becomes illegible. These elaborate letter forms do not fit our computer age.

In the early decades of this century it was common practice to expect children to use metal-tipped pens, liquid ink, and rough-surfaced newsprint for writing exercises. The pen often snagged on the paper fibers on the upstrokes and splattered the paper with ink. In 1922 Marjorie Wise, a concerned English educator, invented a new start-and-stop form of lowercase letters made entirely with downstrokes. To help children avoid ink blots, she separated lowercase letters into separate strokes, like capitals. Teachers sometimes refer to these letters as the *ball-stick* method, or simply *manuscript* (Figure 9). This has been the most common form of letters taught to American beginning writers since 1922 (Gray, 1979).

Unfortunately, Wise didn't realize she was creating the same problems children have with capital letters: start-and-stop letters require young children to determine which direction to go with each new stroke. Within two years Wise found so many handwriting problems developing, especially reversals, that she urged teachers to return to lowercase letters made with continuous lines instead of separate strokes (Connard, 1935). The rest of the world returned to chancery cursive forms for beginners. However, American teachers and publishers continued to use the ball-stick method.

The result has been two generations of American children

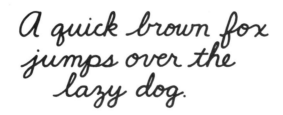

Figure 7. Joined cursive

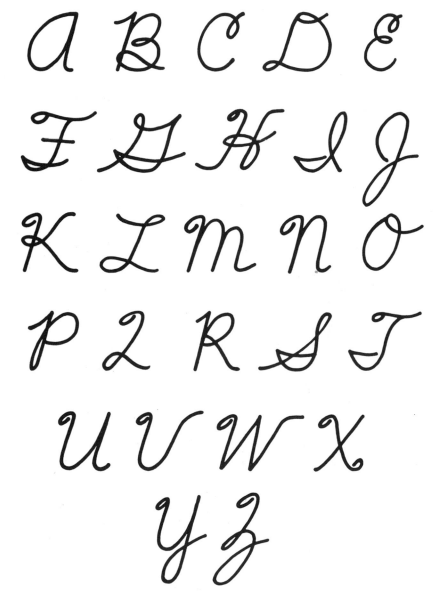

Figure 8. Baroque capitals

a b c d e f
g h i j k
l m n o p
q r s t u
v w x y z

Figure 9. Ball-stick or manuscript alphabet

who frequently make letter reversals and many young children who are unnecessarily labeled "perceptually handicapped" or "weak in fine-motor development." Such problems are compounded by the trend toward lower school entrance age and by the higher curriculum expectations for today's kindergarten and first-grade children.

This is why so many American adults' writing is so difficult to read. Doctors claim that their writing is illegible because they had to write so fast in medical school. Doctors in other countries have legible writing because they were not taught first with ball-stick forms, then switched to archaic cursive forms which became illegible with speed.

In recent years chancery cursive forms have been revived by Donald Neal Thurber in a form called D'Nealian handwriting. When made with *continuous* lines—not lifting the writing tool until each letter is completed—lowercase letters in chancery cursive or italic do not require so many directional decisions. Piaget (1971) tells us that the "pre-operational" child (usually under six) solves movement problems with "perceptual" rather than "rational" intuition. The young child is more aware of a whole design than of its parts. The most important advantage of a continuous-line alphabet for beginners is that a second, different alphabet does not have to be learned in a later grade.

In a further effort to decide which form of letters to use with very young children, I devised the following difficulty scale to determine mathematically which forms are easiest to make (Figure 10). Every difficulty factor adds a point toward the difficulty sum for each individual letter.

Following this scale, capitals add up to 327 in difficulty (Figure 11).

Chancery cursive and the common ball-stick manuscript are similar to each other in difficulty, 300 and 301 (Figure 12).

Of these lowercase forms, chancery cursive is faster, is less prone to reversals, and lays a strong foundation for later joined words. Also, the difficult diagonal strokes for *k, y,* and *w,* are avoided. On the other hand, five- and six-year-olds, or even younger children attempting to write, usually do not have the neurological control to stop on the fluency "tails" at the end of chancery cursive letters. Instead of ending in a tail, beginners' letters tend to look as if they were followed by the letter *u*. Thus, the letter *u* becomes a *w*.

Difficulty points for strokes that appear in children's scribbles as they mature from age 2 to 6

Additional difficulty points:
**Up-and-down stroke**—1 point for each stroke

**Exactly joined strokes**—1 point per joining

**Tall stick**—1 point

**Descending stroke**—1 point

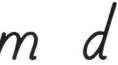

**Tracing over a stroke**—1 point for each stroke

Figure 10. Letter difficulty scale (Based on the
*Beery Developmental Test of Visual-Motor Integration*, 1981)

Figure 11. Difficulty scale for roman capitals

The *itl Integrated Total Language Program* introduces an alternate form for young beginners, based on chancery cursive but simplified by removing any excess strokes and tails. The difficulty scale for this alphabet is only 272 Figure 13). These letters are made even easier for beginners by flattening the tops of left-curve letters *a*, *d*, and *g* (Figure 14). Children will round off these letters as their writing fluency develops.

When made correctly, the simplified forms for the letters *b* and *d* are so different that they are not so easily confused or reversed as in the ball-stick form. Later, young children can be shown how to trace their vertical line for *d* into a perfect chancery cursive *d* when they are ready to learn joined forms (Figure 15).

The *itl* program goes one step further to help beginners differentiate between *b* and *d* by adding the beginnings of the connecting stroke to the *b* at the top of the curve (Figure 16). This provides the foundation for the later joined cursive *b*.

When young children begin with these clear forms of chancery cursive, they need to learn only one set of symbols. With practice, a natural slant develops, circles gradually flat-

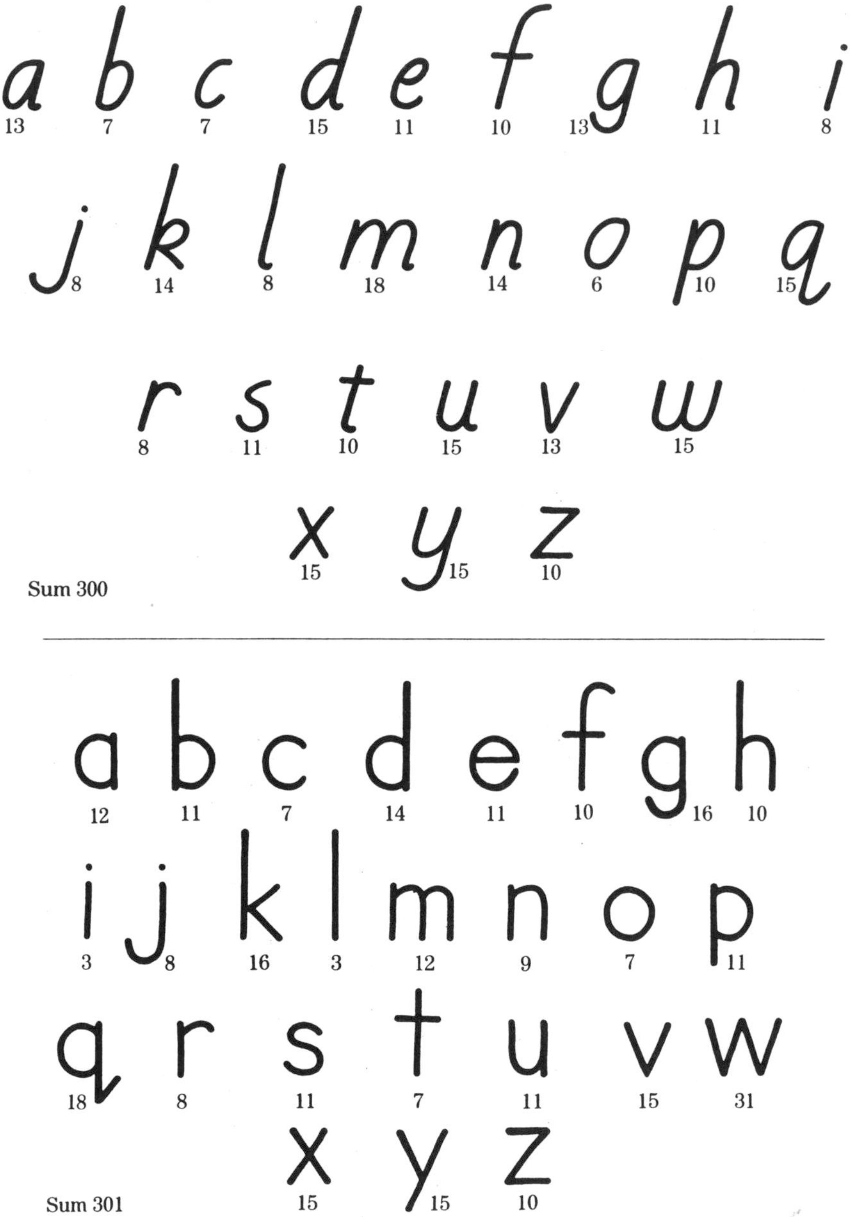

a b c d e f g h i
13  7  7  15  11  10  13  11  8

j k l m n o p q
8  14  8  18  14  6  10  15

r s t u v w
8  11  10  15  13  15

x y z
15  15  10

Sum 300

---

a b c d e f g h
12  11  7  14  11  10  16  10

i j k l m n o p
3  8  16  3  12  9  7  11

q r s t u v w
18  8  11  7  11  15  31

x y z
15  15  10

Sum 301

Figure 12. Difficulty scales for chancery cursive
and ball-stick letters

Figure 13. Difficulty scale for beginner's alphabet
derived from chancery cursive

Figure 14. Simplified left-curve letters with flat top

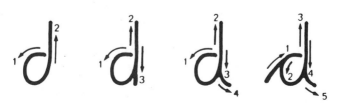

Figure 15. Stages in learning to write chancery cursive *d*

Figure 16. Beginner's Cursive *b*

ten out to ellipses, and some letters naturally join as their fluency tails appear. This form of writing blends pleasingly with roman capitals (Figure 17).

The partly joined form develops naturally and is both fast and legible. Such a personalized writing style is adequate and acceptable to use through adulthood.

Some parents or school boards might insist that the archaic baroque forms also be taught as an art form in the intermediate grades. In this case it would not be necessary to teach a totally new alphabet. Once children are writing fluently in chancery cursive, the two joining strokes, the under curve and the over curve, the new forms for the letters *r* and *s*, and finally, the baroque capitals (Figure 8) can be taught.

## *Letter Sequence*

Children often exhibit their first interest in alphabet letters when they try to copy some of the letters in their name. At this point, it is vital for adults to help children make letters that face in the right direction and follow the correct sequence of strokes. The way letters are first made can become a habit. American parents usually do not hesitate to show their children how to hold a spoon for efficiency, or how to brush their teeth properly. These same parents, however, often hesitate to help young children establish foundation skills for literacy, such as how to hold a crayon or pencil, or how to form letters.

It is not important to start with the first letter when helping children learn to write their names. This is the same fallacy we fall into when we begin to teach the letter *a* first because it is the first letter in an arbitrary alphabet sequence. Children will need to know alphabet order later, when they want to look up a telephone number, or check out

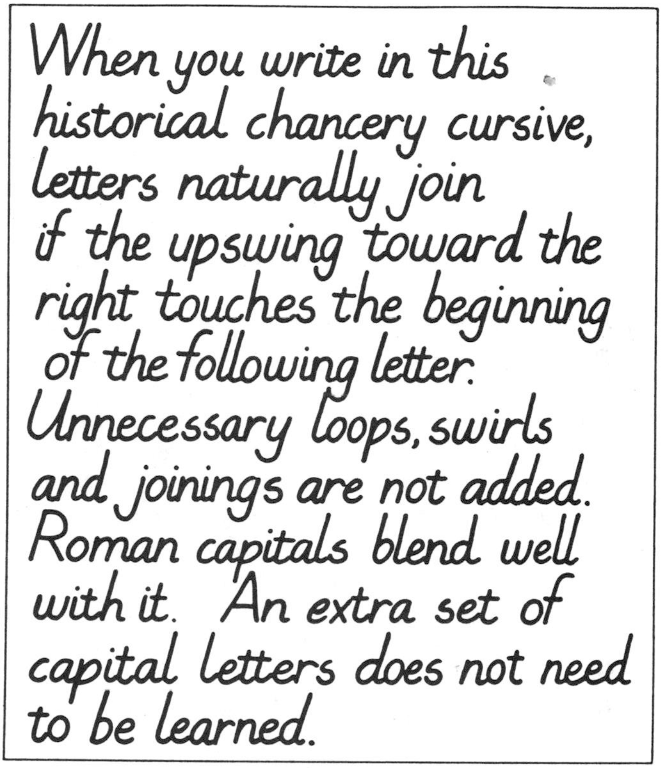

> When you write in this historical chancery cursive, letters naturally join if the upswing toward the right touches the beginning of the following letter. Unnecessary loops, swirls and joinings are not added. Roman capitals blend well with it. An extra set of capital letters does not need to be learned.

Figure 17. Chancery cursive letters with roman capitals

facts in a dictionary or encyclopedia. Certainly it is not harmful to learn the familiar alphabet song. This memory task, however, has no more meaning to beginners than memorizing nursery rhymes whose language is from another era.

When a child shows interest in her or his own name, select the easiest letter in the name to make. The letter charts in "Alphabet Letter Forms" will help determine the difficulty of specific letters. The stroke sequence chart in Appendix D contains information on how to construct letters.

Standing for beginning instruction will help children learn the top-to-bottom patterns of English letters. First, the letter to be learned should be demonstrated to show the stroke sequence. To reinforce the sequence, the child should trace over the lines of the letter in correct stroke sequence, first with the fingertips and then with a writing tool. Then the child should make the letter, once while looking at the model and once without the model. It is important to point out any incorrect sequence of strokes or incorrect direction; poor writing habits are hard to remediate later on. Any letter that approximately resembles the model and is made with the correct stroke sequence and direction should be praised and celebrated.

The child needs to hear the speech sound of the letter. If the child's name is *John*, and the letter is *o*, he has made a picture of "ah." If the child's name is *Joan*, and the letter is o, then, of course, the alphabet name for the letter should be used. Hearing the speech sound in the middle of his or her name and seeing the letter in the middle of the written name will help reinforce learning. (The speech sounds associated with letters are identified in the sound chart in Appendix D.)

When the child can make one letter correctly and say the corresponding sound, then she is ready to write a second letter. Letters that are part of a two-letter speech sound, such as the /ch/ in *Charles* or the /sh/ in *Sharon*, should not be taught until children are making progress with single letters. If the child's name is written with silent letters such as the *h* in *John*, or the *a* in *Joan*, this should be explained to the child.

When a child can write all the letters in her own name, then it is time to concentrate on writing these letters in correct sequence, left to right. If the child begins to write from the right side, she needs to be shown the beginning (left) side. Putting a green dot or a green line on the left side of the paper will help remind beginners where to start. In the *itl Integrated Total Language Program* green stands for *GO*, with the explanation that when we write and read we follow a line from the *Go* side to the *Stop* side of a page. Using the words *left* and *right* will only confuse beginners. *Left*, to young children, is what is left over, and *right* is what is correct. Young children who reverse letters are usually not dyslexic. They usually do not *see* things in mirror image. They simply do not know that our culture arbitrarily has selected left-to-right as the way to write English.

The next step is to go on to other names or other interesting words the child sees, such as those on a favorite cereal box.

My eldest child's interest in letters began at the age of four. One morning he was eating breakfast as I was washing

Sam works on his name with a brush and water on the wall.

dishes. He noticed that a word on his cereal box began with the same letter as the soap I was using. He then commented, "Those letters look the same and they sound the same. Is that how you read?" I assured him that he was on the right track.

When children begin school, teachers often find that many of them have had little or no useful home exposure to letter play. Random teaching of letters then becomes too difficult a task with large groups of children. Some order is necesssary for efficient teaching. The *itl Integrated Total Language Program* has been developed to teach writing in a systematic way.

When helping children to learn a number of unrelated facts, it helps to group the facts in some kind of order and then teach one group at a time (Bugelski, 1964). Multiplication facts are taught this way. Letter teaching is also simplified by breaking the alphabet into manageable groups of letters. In a beginning writing program it makes sense to divide the letters by shape, according to how the symbols are written. Then, for efficiency, the groups can be sequenced according to difficulty. The *itl Integrated Total Language Program* teaches four groups of letters according to their stroke sequence and difficulty: letters that consist of vertical and horizontal lines; left-curve letters; right-curve letters, and letters made with diagonal strokes.

Beery's studies (1981) have given us a strong clue as to how to categorize alphabet letters by shape. Beery did an extensive survey of research studies in visual-motor integration made over a fifty-year period. He deduced the approximate age when each scribble stroke can he imitated or copied by the average child. He then verified the information with an extensive field study of young children's ability to copy forms.

Beery has distinguished between *imitating* and *copying*. *Imitating* means the child observes another doing something first, then does the same thing. The child actually watches the motor act and observes the resulting strokes. *Copying* is a more difficult task, often leading to error. Copying means that the child has only the written letter as a model. When young children are encouraged to copy letters, either at home or school, without being shown the correct direction or sequence of strokes, poor handwriting and dislike of written communication activities often result.

Compare the imitation and copy ages for the first three diagrams on the Beery scale (Figure 18). You can show a child how to make a stroke sooner than she or he can figure out how to do it. Also, by teaching correct top-to-bottom, left-to-right direction, you lay the foundation for making letters.

Beery's age-related scale shows that the easiest letters to make are those made only with vertical and horizontal lines, without exact joining of strokes: *i, t,* and *l.* The letter *j* is sim-

|  | | Imitate* | Copy |
|---|---|---|---|
| vertical line | \| | 1 year 9 months | 2 years 10 months |
| horizontal line | — | 2 years 6 months | 3 years 0 months |
| closed line | ◯ | 2 years 9 months | 3 years 0 months |
| vertical-horizontal cross | + | | 4 years 1 month |
| diagonal toward left | ⟋ | | 4 years 4 months |
| square | ◻ | | 4 years 6 months |
| diagonal toward right | ⟍ | | 4 years 7 months |

*There is no imitation scale after the closed line.

Figure 18. Beery Scale

ply *i* with a tail curling toward the "*GO*" side. The letter *o* should also be easy to teach.

The most difficult letters to make. according to Beery, are those containing the slant stroke toward the right side: *x* and *v* and the capitals *A, W, M, N, K,* and *Y.* If the ball-stick manuscript form of letters is used, then *w, k,* and *y* are also in the "most difficult" group. The letter *k* is the hardest letter to make in capital or manuscript form because it requires a diagonal going in and then out. The letter *z* is also difficult because of the three changes in direction. Olson (1970) states that the difficulty of making diagonal lines lies in their moving in two directions at once, up or down and left or right.

Another group of letters is made with circles and parts of circles combined with vertical lines. The major problem in teaching the writing of these letters is the young child's undeveloped knowledge of left and right on objects outside the body. It makes sense to teach these letters in two separate groups, those that curve left and those that curve right. This strategy tends to avoid the directionality problem. It also helps to point out to young children that most of the right-curve letters begin with a "stick."

Separating the letters *b* and *d*, the two most commonly confused letters, into two teaching groups tends to cut down on their reversal. Twenty years of observing young children making curved letters has convinced me that it is the direction of the beginning of the first stroke that is most important. As one five-year-old put it, "I know where to start, but I don't know which way I'm going!" She was trying to write her name, *Mary*, in start-and-stop manuscript form. In addition to the difficult capital *M* and the final *y* with two different slants, she also had to contend with the left-curve *a* and the right-curve *r*.

If a child starts a letter correctly, she or he is more likely to execute the rest of it without error. If a whole group of letters begins in the same direction, it makes sense to teach those letters together so that learning the one key stroke will make it easier to learn others that start the same way. There will be fewer left-right decisions to make.

The child can also "talk through" a problem, starting with a known and going to the unknown by adding a stroke; for example: "*c* turns into *d*," and "*r* turns into *n*."

The group of letters that begins with left curves and the group that is made with verticals and right curves are of similar difficulty. The left-curve group, however, appears more frequently in English. It contains three of the vowels and the important letter *d*. Two surveys point out that the letter *d* appears more than twice as often as *b* in primary vocabulary, both in textbooks and in children's books (Barnes and Barnes, 1972; Durr, 1973). If children learn left-curve letters first, they will be able to make more primary-level words than they will with right curves.

This sequence of letter groups, therefore, seems to be developmentally sound:

1. *i t l* (vertical and horizontal lines)
2. *j c a d f g o s e* (left curves)
3. *u r n h m p b (y w k)* (right curves)
4. *th ch sh qu ng* (combinations)
5. *x y z (y w k)* (diagonal strokes)

It is not important to follow the letter sequence within each group exactly. What is important, however, is to be aware of the levels of difficulty. Because a feeling for left and right is not an automatic reflex in young children, the two groups of curves should certainly be separated. If the ballstick manuscript form is followed, the *w, y,* and *k* should not be taught until the child is ready to work on the difficult letters with diagonal strokes. If continuous-line lowercase letters are being taught, then the rounded *w, y,* and *k* can be taught with the right-curve letters. Of course, if a child shows interest in learning to make any letter out of sequence, such as those in her or his own name, then by all means take advantage of the child's interest.

The letter *q* should be followed by *u* as a unit. The letter group with *h* should be followed by the combinations with *h* that make new speech sounds *(th, ch, sh)*. These are far more frequent in written English than the diagonal letters in the final group.

## Spelling

In languages such as Italian and Spanish most of the letters represent only one speech sound. Spelling in those languages can be taught simultaneously with beginning reading and writing, making the stage of "invented spelling" unnecessary. Correct *English* spelling, on the other hand, requires learning many rules—and many exceptions to those rules. It isn't reasonable to expect very young children to be able to do this. To spell correctly—according to English dictionary standards— young children would have to learn the spelling patterns of many foreign languages in addition to their own.

Raúl and Ernesto have little trouble
sounding out Spanish words.

### English Spelling

History explains why English spelling is so difficult (Connell, *STAGES*, 1990). The small island of Britain, open on all sides to invaders, was overrun many times in history by conquerors who spoke different languages. Parts of these languages were added to spoken English. Foreign spellings of these additional words have been retained and added to our dictionaries. With the Norman invasion, for example, we acquired variant spellings using the letters *c* and *g*. Words acquired after the invasion use the *gi* and *ge* patterns with the soft /j/ sound (*agile, page*). Words used before the invasion use the hard sound for *g*. These break the rule and must be memorized (*girl, gift*).

Anglo-Saxon scribes used a Celtic, or old Irish, alphabet. The Norman invaders destroyed this regional system of writing in the 11th century. They kept a few necessary Anglo-Saxon letters, but primarily imposed the French alphabet, which had come from Latin. George Reimer (1969), in his book, *How They Murdered the Second R*, expresses it well: "English spelling, as we know it today, was concocted by Anglo-Saxon storytellers, French scribes, and Dutch printers, using an Italian alphabet."

The printing press was invented in the fifteenth century. English, as it was spoken and commonly spelled then, began to be frozen into type. Two problems were created by the early typesetters: The first books printed in English were printed in Holland, and the Dutch printers did not speak English. They not only made spelling errors, but they created their own original spellings. In order to even out their right-hand margins to make them more visually pleasing, they added extra letters to words. Most often this was the letter *e*; the *e* type pieces were conveniently located in front of the operator. Today we repeat their spelling errors and consider them correct.

Adults are sometimes amused by the oddities and inconsistencies of English spelling. For young children, however, English spelling is a cruel system. The biggest problem is that children trying to learn our system often believe that it is they who are wrong, when it is the system that is faulty. Children will not trust people who have deceived them once or twice. How will children learn to trust English spellings that repeatedly trick them? For example, we show young children that we add an *e* at the end of words to cue using the alphabet name sound of the preceding vowel letter; next we expect beginners to read and spell words like *are, come, give,* and *have.*

In addition to a fifteenth-century spelling system that is inconsistent, we have still another spelling problem. Spoken language continually changes. The changes are usually simplifications that reduce the amount of work for the body's speech organs. We then retain the original, phonetically correct spelling words long after we no longer pronounce them to match the spelling. A report by Gelb (1974) discusses the problem:

> The fit between language and writing is generally stronger in the earlier stages of a certain system of writing and weaker in its later stages. This is due to the fact that a writing system when first introduced generally reproduces rather faithfully the underlying phonemic structure. In the course of time, writing, more conservative than language, generally does not keep up with the continuous changes of language, and as time progresses, diverges more and more from its linguistic counterpart.

An example of this progression is that words ending in s are often pronounced today like the letter *z.* This is especially true if the previous letter is voiced by the larynx *(his, dogs, as, is, boys).* It simplifies speaking if we do not constantly alternate between voiced and unvoiced sounds. Spoken language has thus changed, but we keep the original spelling, as if we hissed the final *s.* Written English today uses the *s* letter far more than the *z* letter to indicate the /z/ sound (Dewey 1970). Thus, young, inventive spellers are writing exactly what they hear when they write *wuz.*

The English speech sound /hw/ (as in *hwen, hwere, hwy*) was spelled in reverse by our first Dutch printers and preserved as *wh* in our dictionaries *(when, where, why).* Originally the letter *h* represented a puff of air at the beginning of the word. This speech sound is gradually disappearing in the United States. Listen to American speakers of all dialects on television. Today when is usually pronounced without the /h/ sound as /wen/. The letter h is becoming a spelling convention to be memorized, like the *e* in *are* and *come.*

English spelling is so difficult that there are many literate adults who cannot tell you when to double a consonant, when to use *c, k* or *ck*, or which vowel to use before *r*. If we constantly corrected young children's spoken language, expecting them to talk like college graduates from the beginning, they might soon either stop talking or limit their speech to words and constructions they know for sure. Similarly, if we constantly correct the spelling of beginning writers, they may stop writing or limit themselves to words and constructions that they know.

### Invented Spelling

The young child who writes, *I had spugety for lunch*, has figured out English spelling patterns, but she does not yet know how to spell Italian words, such as *spaghetti*. To do so, she would need to know that in Italian an *h* is used to preserve the hard sound when *g* is followed by *e*, and that in Italian the letter *i* replaces the English final *y*.

The child who writes, *I was sick at home with diureeu*, should get full credit for knowing how to write English.

—He knows how to use the *ck* followisng a short vowel *(sick)*.

—He knows how to cue a long vowel sound with a final *e* *(home)*.

—He has memorized the word *was*, which breaks basic spelling rules.

If the child is mature enough to use a dictionary independently, he can look up the spelling of the Greek-based, Latin-spelled word, *diarrhea*. Until then, his invented phonetic spelling of foreign words should not only be accepted, but celebrated.

Each of a child's original, invented spelling words that can be decoded by another person is proof that the child has learned basic English sound-symbol correspondence. With this knowledge, the child can spell 80 percent of the English primary-level words correctly. The next step in spelling is learning the rules for the remaining 20 percent. It seems logical to help the child learn these rules one at a time as his or her independent writing reveals a need for a particular rule. Finally, the child needs to learn to spell the primary-level words that break these rules. These last works must be memorized. Fortunately, there are not too many of them. Adults who misspell words are usually individuals who either do not know the basic phonetic system of English, or the basic

I wocht the nutckrackr bala.

Seanna (5) can write two sounds for the letter *a* with *bala*. The French spelling *ballet* is not developmentally appropriate.

primary spelling rules, or both. They try to write by visual memory, and the memory load is too great.

### Spelling Levels

Three current researchers in the field of spelling agree that beginning spelling should be taught as a system—not a perfect system, like math, but nevertheless a system (Henderson, 1985; Gentry, 1984; Read, 1986).

When parents express concern about invented spelling it helps to show them the five levels that can be observed when children begin to write:

1. **Precommunicative:** letters strung together with an obvious lack of understanding that letters represent speech sounds.
2. **Semi-phonetic:** some speech sounds represented. Alphabet letter names are sometimes used to represent whole syllables or even whole words, especially the letters *R* and *U*. We are amused by adults' spelling like this on vanity license plates. One child's

Level 1 spelling
Brandi can write letters but does not associate
them with speech sounds yet.

Level 2 spelling
Dylan shows phonemic awareness and begins to associate letters
with speech sounds. ("I was sitting by a tree.")

Level 3 spelling
Peter (5) writes "knock-knock" jokes. His invented spelling can
easily be translated. He uses both a question mark and a period.

Level 4 spelling
Brenna (6) knows that there is a *w* in *strawberry*, but she
is not sure where to put it.

Level 5 spelling
Kirsten (5) has spelled all English words correctly. Foreign words,
like *spaghetti*, are not developmentally appropriate.

first meaningful writing was in protest when his
mother was not paying attention to him. He had written, *RUDF* (Are you deaf?) (Bissex, 1980).

3. **Phonetic:** all speech sounds are represented, but
   spellings are often invented. The samples of kindergarten children's writing in this book (pages 60-63)
   are already at this third level.

4. **Transitional:** correct letters, but incorrect sequence.
   When students begin to read, they sometimes try to
   remember visual patterns, but fail to put letters in
   the right order.

5. **Correct:** This does not mean dictionary correct, but
   developmentally correct. For example, if a spelling
   rule has not been taught, then it should not be
   expected. The children's captions on this page and
   page 98 are correct at the kindergarten or first grade
   level. There is no reason to expect correct spelling of
   *spaghetti* or *ballet*, neither of which is spelled follow-

ing English patterns. Until children are reading at least at middle second grade level they do not have the skills to look up such words in a dictionary.

Teachers should keep a portfolio of samples of each student's writings to demonstrate to the child, the parents, and possibly an administrator the gradual growth in spelling in these five levels.

### Suggestions for Helping Beginners

When helping young children with spelling, we need to remember that they are not adults. When adults write, they silently dictate to themselves. Young children, however, need to bring all their senses to the task. When they begin to want to write independently, young children need to say the words aloud, listen to themselves as they write each sound, and feel the position of the mouth for each sound. Their first writing is noisy self-dictation, just as adult writing is silent self-dictation.

The major problem for beginners is that spoken speech, even their own, is usually too rapid for their ears to sort out the speech sounds in sequence. One way to encourage young children to listen to themselves talk is to have them listen for a specific sound in a word. For example, give children a sheet of paper divided into three columns and tell them to listen for a sound; "Listen for /m/." Ask children to repeat the sound aloud. Then tell them to listen carefully to decide whether the /m/ is at the beginning, middle, or end of the words you say. Dictate a list of words, such as *him, tummy, gum*. Tell children to repeat the word and feel the /m/ on their lips. Then tell them to write the letter *m* in the appropriate column.

Another game that helps children sort out sounds by ear is to play *robot-talk*, varying the speed of your speech. Talk very slowly at first. For example, say a familiar multisyllable word, such as *ham-bur-ger*, very slowly. Then challenge children to say the word fast. Use familiar words at first, such as *fan-tas-tic*. Then try nonsense words, such as *gob-ble-de-gook*, or *plum-did-dle*. When children can play this game successfully, using only ear and voice, then let a child be the robot and say words slowly for you to repeat rapidly. Use words from languages other than English (*mu-cha-cho*), especially if there are children in your group whose native language is not

English. This is a game that all can play because meaning is not required for success.

When slow-talk and fast-talk have been learned, play the game with single sounds of short words rather than syllables. Begin with two-letter words that start with a vowel (i-n, a-t). Graduate to three-letter words beginning with consonant sounds that can continue on a breath (/f/, /l/, /m/, /n/, /r/, /s/, /v/, /z/). Then add the more difficult consonant sounds that are momentarily stopped in the mouth and then explode into sound (/b/, /c/, /d/, /j/, /g/, /p/, and /t/). (See the Phonics Guide on pages 71–72 for information on speech sounds.) Say words slowly for children to repeat at normal speed *(f-a-t, m-a-n, s-i t, z-i-p)*. Then make it even more fun by adding "outer-space language." Make up nonsense words *(t-a-f, n-o-m, l-u-p, r-e-v)*.

Your eventual goal is to help young children listen to themselves self-dictate as they write. At first you will probably need to listen to a child's words and repeat each word slowly, sound by sound. Hold up one finger for each speech sound as you say it. Then ask the child to repeat the sounds in sequence, slowly. Finally the child should be expected to write the corresponding letters in left-to-right sequence, saying each speech sound as the corresponding letter is written. Eventually the child will be able to self-dictate without help.

If a child writes *mik* for *milk*, hold up four fingers, one at a time, and repeat the sounds, /m//i//l//k/. Ask the child to imitate you, repeating the sounds and holding up one finger at a time. The child will discover the missing sound and letter and make her own correction. This is the start of independent proofreading. If, on the other hand, a young beginner writes *milc* for *milk*, accept it at first until the child either discovers the error by studying a milk carton, or until you have taught the spelling rules for *c, k,* and *ck*. If children continually ask, "How do you spell _____?", lead them to try to do it independently, using voice and ears. It will help children to know that learning to spell is a separate skill from learning to write.

About 80 percent of our language is based on the Old English spelling patterns agreed upon by the Anglo-Saxon forebears of the English people. They are the easiest to learn to write and spell, because they are, like Spanish and Italian, based on a simple system of one-to-one sound-symbol correspondence. These are the spelling patterns primarily covered by the *itl Integrated Total Language Program.* (A list of easy practice words is in Appendix A.) If a beginner makes errors in these words, reversing letters or words, or substituting one letter for another, the child should be reminded that written English letters and words go from left to right, with each speech sound and letter following the other. If necessary, continue to draw a green line down the left side of the paper to indicate the *GO,* or starting side, of all words.

We do not expect beginners in instrumental music to play a concerto, or beginners in swimming to demonstrate a variety of strokes. It is foolish to expect beginning writers to spell all words correctly. On the other hand, it is just as foolish to accept spelling errors on the premise that the child's creativity will be thwarted. Some children will continue to use invented spelling as long as they are permitted to do so. Timing is the answer. For example, when children have been shown that in order to make the letters *a, e, i, o,* and *u* represent their alphabet names, one must usually add a cue, they should be expected to use the cues in independent writing. At first, the beginner should be expected to add any extra vowel until the practice of adding *something* is established. After the long-vowel rule has been taught, *rite* but not *rit* should be accepted. Children shouldn't be expected to use *right* or *write* until about the beginning of third grade in most American schools. Similarly, after the long-vowel rule has been taught in first grade, *road* or *rode* should be accepted, but not *rod.* Children may not distinguish between these two words until about third grade. The task of writing will be too difficult and children will begin to resist any writing assignment if unrealistic spelling expectations are placed on their independent writing.

For the 20 percent of English words that are not spelled with simple sound-symbol correspondence, add the basic primary spelling rules of English one at a time until they are mastered. (See Appendix B.) It takes about two years to cover them. About the middle of first grade, children will begin to encounter some reading words that break most of these spelling rules. Then they can be taught to use a good beginning dictionary, with only primary-level words, to check the spelling of these deviant words. Knowing that good writers check their spelling all the time will be encouraging to children. (The most frequently used "outlaw" words, that must eventually be memorized, are listed in Appendix C.)

# APPENDIXES

## Appendix A
### Easiest Words for Beginning Spellers

The following words serve as patterns for spelling 80 percent of English primary-level words. All of these words are taught in the *itl Integrated Total Language Program*. They follow the sequence of the five letter groups on page 93.

These words are similar in level of spelling difficulty, with the obvious difference that two-letter words are easier than three-letter words. They are divided into four groups according to writing difficulty. When teaching children to spell, encourage them to "sound-spell," uttering each speech noise as they write the corresponding letter.

When children are starting to write, attempts to call letters by their alphabet names should be discouraged. Children are learning to coordinate sensory mechanisms (ear, hand, eye) to function at full capacity in the writing act. Alphabet names will halt fluency.

Occasionally asking children to write a nonsense word will help determine whether they have just memorized the words, or whether they are learning the sound-symbol system. (Nonsense words are in italics.)

### Level 1
it
lit
*il*
*til*

## Level 2

| | | | |
|---|---|---|---|
| is | *jit* | cot | dig |
| as | *lij* | dad | dog |
| at | cat | did | dot |
| fat | get | sag | dads |
| *tac* | got | tag | lads |
| *tif* | let | jog | test |
| fed | lid | jig | glad |
| fit | sad | dogs | flag |
| fog | sat | cats | |
| gas | sit | cots | |

## Level 3

| | | | |
|---|---|---|---|
| am | net | has | mad |
| an | nip | hat | rip |
| and | on | hen | rob |
| ant | pad | hid | sun |
| bad | dip | him | tan |
| bed | end | his | tap |
| cab | fan | hit | ten |
| bud | fin | hot | tin |
| can | fun | hug | up |
| cut | pal | hum | kid |
| den | pat | in | yes |
| dim | pan | pip | wet |
| men | pen | pot | yet |
| man | pig | rag | us |
| met | pit | run | jug |
| mom | pin | rat | *tig* |
| mat | gum | ran | tug |
| mop | had | *maj* | dust |
| mug | ham | red | rod |
| mud | *dap* | jam | rats |
| *mid* | *pid* | job | rugs |
| *dum* | *naf* | lip | hand |
| *pom* | *nep* | *nus* | stop |
| nap | | | |

## Level 4

| | | | |
|---|---|---|---|
| quit | sang | thin | ship |
| this | bong | with | fish |
| that | lung | chin | shin |

| chip | them | chop | gang |
|------|------|------|------|
| dish | than | wish | |

## Level 5

van
box
six
zip
mix
*mux*
*zop*

## Appendix B

## Primary Spelling Rules*

English spelling rules have a number of common exceptions. Nevertheless, there are generalities that work. These are especially valuable to help young children whose visual and auditory memories are not sufficiently developed to be successful with traditional school spelling methods. These spelling patterns, called *rules* here, can be used to help school-age children accept the inconsistencies of English spelling—to make sense of it. They should not be taught to very young children (under first grade) unless a child asks why a particular word doesn't look like it sounds. (Children who resist rules may be more accepting if you refer to the rules as "clues for solving the spelling puzzles.")

The words used as examples are the most frequently found words in children's first writings. They are also the most frequently used words in first- and second-grade basal readers and children's books.

Explain a rule to a single school-age child or to a group when the need arises. This may be when you observe that the spellings of particular words are difficult to decode. If, for example, you observe errors like, *The citten played with the ball,* you will know that it is time to demonstrate Rule 15, for *c* and *k*. When you observe *me* spelled *my*, then help children use Rules 1 and 5. Most children can learn and apply these spelling rules by the end of second grade, provided the rules are taught and practiced. They should not be taught, however, until children can spell the easy word patterns in Appendix A correctly.

---

*The spelling patterns in this appendix apply to words most frequently used in primary writing and reading materials.

## Rule 1

When *o, e,* or *i* are all alone, or stand at the end of a one-syllable word, we say they are *open*. There is no final consonant to close them off, as in the common English "sandwich" pattern (consonant-vowel-consonant). When the final consonant "gate" has been removed, the vowel letter can run away and shout its own alphabet name.

| | |
|---|---|
| go | she |
| so | be |
| no | I |
| he | hi |
| me | |

Exceptions to this rule:

| | |
|---|---|
| see | do |
| free | who |
| three | snow |
| to | blow |

## Rule 2

Words ending in the alphabet name sound for the letter *a* are exceptions to Rule 1. These usually add a *y* letter.

| | |
|---|---|
| day | away |
| play | today |
| may | |

## Rule 3

For words not covered by Rules 1 and 2, we add an extra vowel as the cue to help the letters *a, e, i,.o,* or *u* represent their alphabet names. Sometimes the extra vowel follows the letter. Sometimes it is an *e* at the end of the word.

| *a* | *i* | *o* |
|---|---|---|
| make | five | home |
| made | nine | boat |
| | fire | four |
| | ride | |
| *e* | die | |
| eat | | *u* |
| dear | | use |
| green | | blue |
| read | | |
| here | | |

*Rule 4*

Double the consonant following the vowel, if you do not want a vowel to say its alphabet name in words of more than one syllable.

| | |
|---|---|
| daddy | happy |
| little | rabbit |
| apple | |

The opposite rule also works. Do *not* double the consonant following the vowel if you want it to say its alphabet name.

baby
begin
open
table

*Rule 5*

The letter *y* represents the letter name for *i* on the end of single-syllable words.

| | |
|---|---|
| my | dry |
| sky | cry |
| by | why |

Variations that children need to learn early:

hi
pie
tie

*Rule 6*

Vowels before the letter *r* are especially tricky. There are some basic generalities in primary vocabulary that will help:

The letter *o* says its alphabet name before *r*, with slight dialectical variations.

or
for

The letter *a* changes its sound to /ah/ before *r*.

| | |
|---|---|
| car | bark |
| far | dark |
| arm | |

The letters *i* and *e* are almost "silent" before *r*. At the end of words, we often add an *e* before *r*.

| | |
|---|---|
| her | ever |
| mother | never |
| after | |

When the speech sound /r/ is heard in the middle of words, it is usually preceded by the letter *i*.

| | |
|---|---|
| bird | dirt |
| first | girl |
| shirt | |

Primary-word exceptions, where *u* precedes *r* in the middle of words, should be memorized.

| | |
|---|---|
| fur | nurse |
| purple | hurt |
| burn | |

Many words beginning with *w* are exceptions to the previous *r* rules.

word
world
work
water

*Rule 7*

In two-vowel combinations, both vowels are sometimes pronounced. These two-vowel combinations are called *diphthongs*. Diphthongs often use the letters *w* and *y* as vowel sounds.

| | |
|---|---|
| boy | brown |
| toy | how |
| out | cow |
| our | now |

*Rule 8*

English words never end in *v*. Add an *e* whether the preceding vowel is short or long.

live
give
have

*Rule 9*

The digraph *ch* is preceded by *t* following short vowels.

catch
itch
witch

This is not true with long vowels.

each

*Rule 10*
Spelling patterns for *au, aw, all, old, igh, ind, ild* don't follow the rules and need to be memorized by the end of second grade.

| | |
|---|---|
| saw | find |
| all | behind |
| ball | old |
| call | cold |
| fall | child |

*Rule 11*
The *h* letter is silent in most words that begin with *wh*. Use *wh* to begin most of the question words. *Who* is spelled the same way, but pronounced with a silent *w*. *Where* and *what* are "outlaw" words and need to be memorized. (See Appendix C.)

when
why
white
who

*Rule 12*
Every English *syllable* must have one of these vowel letters: *a, e, i, o, u,* or *y*. The word *two* adds an *o*. The word *new* adds an *e*. Words ending in a syllable pronounced /ul/ or /l/ always add an *e* after the *l*.

two
new
apple
little

*Rule 13*
Double the *l* or *f* at the end of short-vowel, single-syllable words.

| | |
|---|---|
| off | ill |
| tell | will |
| bell | till |
| sell | doll |

*Rule 14*
The unstressed prefix /uh/ is usually spelled with the letter *a*, like the article, *a*.

| | |
|---|---|
| away | asleep |
| about | a |
| ago | |

*Rule 15*
For the /k/ sound, use *c* before *a, o,* or *u*. Use *k* before *i* or *e*.

| | |
|---|---|
| cat | kitten |
| cot | kite |
| cut | make |

Use *ck* after a short vowel.

black
sick
back
duck

Use only a *k* instead of a *ck* at the end of words if the /k/ sound is preceded by a consonant instead of a vowel. The second consonant takes the place of the *c* in *ck*.

milk
dark
ask

*Rule 16*
Use the letter *c*, when followed by *i, e,* or *y*, to represent the /s/ sound.

ice
mice
face
city

*Rule 17*
Use the letter *g*, when followed by *i, e,* or *y*, to represent the /j/ sound.

age
huge
orange

## Appendix C
## Outlaw Words

These common primary words don't follow any of the previous spelling rules. They are listed in order of their frequency of appearance in both children's early writing and in primary-level books. Correct spelling for these words needs to be memorized early, certainly by the end of third grade (Durr, 1973).

| First Grade | Second Grade | Third Grade |
|---|---|---|
| the | gone | write |
| to | pull | right |
| a | some | about |
| you | come | would |
| said | want | walk |
| was | where | their |
| they | any | once |
| do | many | because |
| one | were | please |
| there | does | eight |
| your | been | |
| look | what | |
| book | add | |
| good | buy | |
| love | done | |
| put | father | |
| school | full | |
| of | house | |
| from | city | |
| are | | |

## Appendix D
## Letter and Sound Charts

The following letter forms, described in "Alphabet Letter Forms" in Part 2, are grouped according to writing difficulty. The thirty symbols and combinations of symbols represent all the basic speech sounds of American English. The sequence of sounds and letters is the same one used in the *itl Integrated Total Language Program.*

This chart is intended as a guide for adults who are helping young children learn to write, not for children to copy.

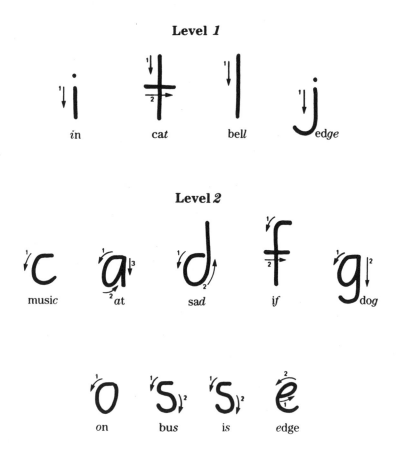

Level *1*

in     cat     bell     edge

Level *2*

music     at     sad     if     dog

on     bus     is     edge

## Level 3

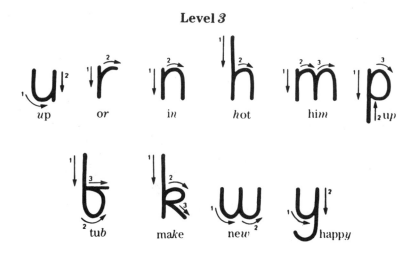

up  or  in  hot  him  up

tub  make  new  happy

## Level 4

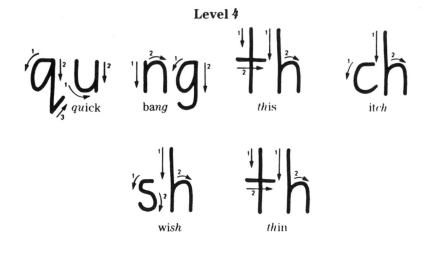

quick  bang  this  itch

wish  thin

## Level 5

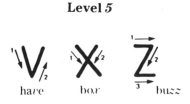

have  box  buzz

# Appendix E
## Progress Checklist

This checklist may he used to record children's progress from early scribbling through writing and saying the symbols and sounds of the English language. The first nine items are prewriting skills. The remaining items correspond to the sequence used in the *itl Integrated Total Language Program* and described in Appendix D.

___ Draws vertical lines
___ Draws horizontal lines
___ Draws closed-line circles or ovals
___ Draws stripes inside closed-line shapes
___ Draws vertical-horizontal crosses
___ Draws closed-line shapes, stripes extending outside perimeter
___ Draws closed-line shapes with empty centers and rays on perimeter (suns)
___ Draws primitive face (circle with eyes)
___ Draws and *names* person
___ Writes $i, t, l$, and $j$ from dictation of their speech sounds
___ Tells sounds for letters $i, t, l$, and $j$
___ Writes $c, a, d, f, g, o, s$, and $e$ from dictation of their speech sounds
___ Tells sounds for letters $c, a, d, f, g, o, s$, and $e$
___ Writes regularly spelled words from dictation using letters $i, t, l, j, c, a, d, f, g, o, s$, and $e$
___ Writes $u, y, w, r, n, h, p, b, m$, and $k$ from dictation of their speech sounds
___ Tells sounds for letters $u, y, w, r, n, h, p, b, m$, and $k$
___ Writes regularly spelled words from dictation using all previously learned letters
___ Writes $qu, th, ch, sh$, and $ng$ from dictation of their speech sounds
___ Tells sounds for $qu, th, ch, sh$, and $ng$
___ Writes regularly spelled words from dictation using all previously learned letters
___ Writes $v, x$, and $z$ from dictation of their speech sounds
___ Tells sounds for $v, x$, and $z$

___ Writes regularly spelled words from dictation using all previously learned letters

___ Tells alphabet names for *a, e, i, o,* and *u*

___ Writes long-vowel words from dictation adding a second vowel to cue its sound

___ Reads sound-controlled readers

___ Reads books of own selection using variant vowels

___ Writes all capital letters

___ Tells alphabet names for letters in any random order

___ Recites alphabet order in correct sequence

## Appendix F

## The NAPA Comparative Study (Connell, 1975)

### Population

*Students:* All kindergarten students enrolled in the Napa
Valley (California) Unified School District in 1974–75 were
included in this study (994 students). There is little zoning of
housing in the school district, either in urban or rural areas.
There are no specific "pockets of poverty." The schools are
naturally integrated and statistically comparable. In 1970,
the last year when it was legal to give group intelligence tests
in California schools, the median district IQ was 102. The
range among schools was 100 to 104.

*Teachers:* Teachers volunteered to participate in the study in
return for a set of materials. Nineteen classes formed the
experimental *itl* group. Twenty-six classes formed the control
group. The two groups of teachers ranged in age from 26 to
55. Their median age was 40. Their teaching experience
ranged from 3 years to 20 years. For evaluation purposes, the
director of elementary education and the director of personnel checked personnel files. The data indicated that the 19
participating teachers and the 26 nonparticipating teachers
were as comparable in age and experience as human variabil-
ity permits.

### Procedures

The 19 experimental classes used the *itl* program with its
"write-to-read" approach as their major language arts program for the school year (Connell, 1975).

The 26 control classes used a variety of other traditional
published readiness materials of their own choice, including
*DISTAR, Beginning, Alpha Time, Self-Pronouncing Alphabet,*
and others.

### Test Instrument

All children were pretested in October 1974 and posttested in
May 1975 on the *Stanford Early School Achievement Test*
(SESAT I). Only children with both pre- and posttest scores
were compared. All children who scored in the ninth stanine

on the pretest were eliminated from the comparison studies on the premise that there was insufficient ceiling on the test for valid growth scores for them. This left a population of 289 experimental pupils and 460 control pupils.

### Results

1. There was no significant difference between the groups on the item analysis of *Environment* or *Aural Comprehension*.

2. Teaching in the experimental group did not stress letter names, capital letters, or comparison of words with the same beginning sounds. Teaching in some control groups did emphasize these activities. The experimental group, therefore, was disadvantaged on the *Letters and Sounds* item, which tests this knowledge. In spite of this disadvantage, the experimental group results were favorable.

## Letters and Sounds:
*Median Growth in Raw Scores*

| | |
|---|---|
| Experimental | 8.62 |
| Control | 8.02 |
| Difference | 7.5% |

3. Scott (1968) points up the relationship between math skills and beginning reading. He reports that seriation alone is more predictive of later reading success than other traditional reading readiness measures. Whimbey and Whimbey (1975), in their study of the development of intelligence, show that the ability to make logical analysis of facts is the common skill that is transferable from one subject to another.

The teaching of letters in sequence to form words contributed to higher math scores in the experimental group. The difference is significant:

## Math:
*Median Growth in Raw Scores*

| | |
|---|---|
| Experimental | 7.25 |
| Control | 5.58 |
| Difference | 30% |

4. Children scoring at stanine eight or nine on the SESAT I posttests were also administered the *Word Reading* and *Sentence Reading* components of SESAT II. A total of 245 students took the SESAT II posttest to determine how many kindergarten students could actually read at the end of the school year. The difference strongly favored the experimental group:

*Median Growth in Raw Scores*

|  | **Word Reading** | **Sentence Reading** |
|---|---|---|
| Experimental | 43 | 13.3 |
| Control | 36 | 9 |
| Difference | 19% | 47% |

5. Particular attention was paid to classes whose median pretest scores were below the 52nd percentile. There were four of these low classes in both the experimental and control groups, in spite of the original assumption that all kindergarten classes would enter school with similar potential.

The four experimental classes with the lowest scores at entrance (total raw scores in pretest) produced 40 students who scored at the ninth stanine on the posttest. The four comparable control classes produced 20 pupils who scored at the ninth stanine on the posttest. These 60 pupils took SESAT II with these significant results:

*Median Growth in Raw Scores*

|  | **Word Reading** | **Sentence Reading** |
|---|---|---|
| Experimental | 29 | 5 |
| Control | 10 | 1.6 |
| Difference | 190% | 213% |

# REFERENCES

Adams, Marilyn Jager. *Beginning to Read*. Cambridge: MIT Press, 1990.

Aitchison, Jean. *The Articulate Mammal*. New York: Universe Books, 1976.

Barnes, Albert Jr., and Nancy Barnes. "An Examination of the Dolch Basic Sight Vocabulary in the California State-Adopted Primary Spelling, Primary Reading, and Primary English Series." *California Journal of Educational Research* (September 1972).

Beery, Keith. *Revised Test of Visual-Motor Integration*. Chicago: Follett Publishing, 1981.

Bissex, Glenda. *GNYS AT WRK*. Cambridge: Harvard University Press, 1980.

Bredekamp, Sue. *Developmentally Appropriate Practice in Early Childhood Programs*. Washington D.C.: N.A.E.Y.C., 1987.

Bugelski, B. *The Psychology of Learning Applied to Teaching*. New York: Bobbs-Merrill, 1964.

Chall, Jeanne. *Learning to Read—The Great Debate*. rev. ed. New York: McGraw Hill, 1983.

Chomsky, Carol. "Invented Spelling in First Grade." Paper presented at Reading Research Symposium, State University of New York at Buffalo, 1974.

_____."how sister got into the grog." *Early Years*, November, 1975.

Clay, Marie. *Becoming Literate*. Portsmouth, New Hampshire: Heinemann, 1991.

_____. *Writing Begins at Home*. Aukland, New Zealand: Heinemann, 1987.

Connard, Edith. "The Growth of Manuscript Writing in the United States." *Childhood Education*, January 1935, p. 71.

Connell, Donna. "The Insertion of Writing Skills into Kindergarten Curriculum." Practicum report, Nova University, Fort Lauderdale, 1975.

_____.*itl; Integrated Total Language Program.* Academic Therapy Publications, Inc., 1978; revised 1985 by American Guidance Service, Inc. Now available from Can-Do Books, 2119 Lone Oak Avenue, Napa, CA 94558.

_____. *SLIDE.* East Aurora, New York: D.O.K. Publishers, 1990.

_____. *STAGES* (Sequential Tasks to Assist the Growth of English Spelling). East Aurora, New York: D.O.K. Publishers, 1990.

Coren, Stanley. *The Lefthander Syndrome.* New York. The Free Press, 1992.

Delacato, Carl. *A New Start for the Child with Reading Problems.* New York: David McKay, 1970.

de Quiros, Julio. *Neuropsychological Fundamentals in Learning Disabilities.* Novato, California: Academic Therapy Publications, 1979.

Dewey, Godfrey. *Relative Frequency of English Spellings.* New York Teachers College Press, 1970.

Durkin, Dolores. *Teaching Young Children to Read.* Boston: Allyn & Bacon, 1972.

Durr, William. "Computer Study of High Frequency Words in Popular Trade Juveniles." *The Reading Teacher* (October 1973).

Frankenburg, William, Josiah Dodds, and Alma Fundal, *Denver Developmental Screening Test*, University of Colorado Medical Center, 1972.

Furst, Charles. *Origins of the Mind.* Englewood Cliffs, New Jersey: Prentice Hall, 1979.

Gardner, Howard. *Frames of Mind, The Theory of Multiple Intelligences.* New York: Basic Books, Inc., 1983.

Gelb, I. "Records, Writing, and Decipherment." *Visible Language 8* (1974): 4.

Gentry, J. Richard. "Developmental Aspects of Learning to Spell." Novato, California: *Academic Therapy*, Vol. 20, No. 1, 1984.

Gitter, Lena. *Ready Your Child for School the Montessori Way.* Meinrad, Indiana: St. Meinrad Archabbey, 1969.

Goswami, Usha, and Peter Bryant. *Phonological Skills and Learning to Read.* East Sussex, United Kingdom: Lawrence Erlbaum Associates, 1990.

Graves, Donald, and Virginia Stuart. *Write From the Start*. New York: New American Library, 1985.

Gray, Nicolette. "Towards a New Handwriting Adapted to the Ballpoint Pen." *Visible Language* 13 (1979): 1.

Henderson, Edmund. *Teaching Spelling*. Boston: Houghton Mifflin, 1985.

Hunt, J. McVicker. *Intelligence and Experience*. New York: Roland Press, 1961.

Holdaway, Don. *The Foundations of Literacy*. Sydney, Australia: Ashton Scholastic, 1979.

Ibuka, Masaru. *Kindergarten Is Too Late*. New York: Simon and Schuster, 1977.

Johnson, D. "An Investigation of Sex Differences in Reading in Four English-Speaking Nations." Technical Report no. 209, Wisconsin Research and Development Center, 1972.

Kaufman, Barry Neil. *Son-Rise*. New York: Warner Books, 1977.

Kellogg, Rhoda. *Analyzing Children's Art*. Palo Alto, California: National Press Books, 1969–70.

Koffka, K. *The Growth of the Mind*. Paterson, New Jersey: Littlefield Adama, 1959.

Lerch, Harold, John Becker, Bonnie Ward, and Judith Nelson. *Perceptual Motor Learning—Theory and Practice*. Palo Alto, California: Peck, 1974.

Lillard, P, *Montessori, A Modern Approach*. New York: Schocken Books, 1972.

Maccoby, Eleanor, and Carol Jacklin. *The Psychology of Sex Differences*, Palo Alto, California: Stanford University Press, 1974.

McBroom, Patricia. "Mining the Child's Art." *Science News* 93 (1968): 27.

McKean, Kevin. "Beaming New Light on the Brain." *Discover 2* (December 1981): 30–33.

Montessori, Maria. *The Discovery of the Child*. New York: Fides Publishers, 1967.

Olds, J. "Ten Milliseconds into the Brain: A First Sketch of the Path of Learning." *Psychology Today* (1975): 45–48.

Olson, David. *Cognitive Development, The Child's Acquisition of Diagonality*. New York: Academic Press, 1970.

Olson, Janet. *Envisioning Writing*. Portsmouth, New Hampshire: Heinemann, 1992.

Piaget, Jean. *The Child's Conception of Movement and Speed*, New York: Ballantine Books, 1971.

Platt, Penny. "Grapho-linguistics: Children's drawings in relation to reading and writing skills." *The Reading Teacher*, December 1977.

Pulaski, Mary Ann Spencer. *Understanding Piaget*. New York: Harper & Row, 1971.

Read, Charles. *Children's Creative Spelling*. London: Routledge & Kegan Paul, 1986.

Reimer, George. *How They Murdered the Second R*. New York: W. W. Norton, 1969.

Scott, R. "Perceptual Readiness as a Predictor of Success in Reading." *Reading Teacher* 22 (1968): 36–39.

Stanford Achievement Test Series. SESAT 1, SESAT 2. New York: Harcourt Brace Jovanovich, 1983.

Thomas, James. *Introduction to Human Embryology*. Philadelphia: Lea Febiger, 1968.

Travis, Lee. *Handbook of Speech Pathology*. New York: Appleton Century Crofts, 1978.

Whimbey, A., and L. Whimbey. *Intelligence Can Be Taught*. New York: E.P. Dutton, 1975.

Winitz, Harris. *Articulatory Acquisition and Behavior*. New York: Appleton Century Crofts, 1969.